Finding Virtue's Place

∽

Finding Virtue's Place

Examining America's Civic Life

∽

S. Lance Denning

PRAEGER

Westport, Connecticut
London

Library of Congress Cataloging-in-Publication Data

Denning, S. Lance, 1961–
   Finding virtue's place : examining America's civic life / S.
Lance Denning.
    p. cm.
  Includes bibliographical references (p.   ) and index.
  ISBN 0–275–96459–0 (alk. paper)
  1. Political participation—United States. 2. Civil
society—United States. I. Title.
  JK1764.D49 1999
  323'.042'0973—dc21   99–34440

British Library Cataloguing in Publication Data is available.

Library of Congress Catalog Card Number: 99–34440
ISBN: 0–275–96459–0

First published in 1999

Praeger Publishers, 88 Post Road West, Westport, CT 06881
An imprint of Greenwood Publishing Group, Inc.
www.praeger.com

Printed in the United States of America

The paper used in this book complies with the
Permanent Paper Standard issued by the National
Information Standards Organization (Z39.48–1984).

10 9 8 7 6 5 4 3 2 1

Copyright Acknowledgments

The author and publisher gratefully acknowledge permission to reprint the following
material:

Lyrics from the song "Save the Planet" appear courtesy of The Tragically Hip, from the
album *Phantom Power*. Written by The Tragically Hip. © 1998 Wiener Art, Arte Humane,
Dirty Shorts, Bhaji Maker, Ching Music (SOCAN).

Excerpts from *The Radical Politics of Thomas Jefferson: A Revisionist View* by Richard K.
Matthews. Lawrence, Kans.: University Press of Kansas, 1984.

Excerpts throughout, as submitted from *Democracy in America* by Alexis de Tocqueville.
Edited by J. P. Mayer and Max Lerner. Translated by George Lawrence. English transla-
tion copyright © 1965 by Harper & Row, Publishers, Inc. Copyright Renewed. Reprinted
by permission of HarperCollins Publishers, Inc.

for my parents—
for their lasting examples,
and to my nieces and nephews:
Warren and Glen, Leigh and Evan, Isla and Keenan, and Zachary,
for their future civic lives.

Contents

~~

Preface

Burbling below the news flashes of the day, a social tsunami swells. We hear about it most often in the sirens from the Right. A moral decay engulfs society. Divorce erodes families. Crime ebbs ever closer to our backdoors, and the backwaters of permissiveness encourage teen pregnancy, welfare dependency, and drug abuse. Whatever depth of insight the Right offers, their beacons of concern address exclusively America's moral and civic behavior. The Left, if a Left exists these days, counters that economic inequalities and the concentration of wealth exacerbates social tension and moral choices. Crimes decrease if jobs increase. Welfare is not a moral choice, more an economic one. Illicit drug use—as opposed to the socially accepted alcohol and tobacco use—decreases when a safe environment and the prospects for a professional career demand a youth's time and energy.

The battle lines are thus drawn. The Right focuses on America's decrepit morality and cries out for an infusion of character. The Left demands greater commitments to economic policies that nurture education and employment to overcome poverty, homelessness, and the more widespread squeeze on middle-class families. The outcome from these battles is well established. Since both enunciate legitimate concerns and real dangers, both positions state valid points. But American politics demands a winner and a loser, and most often the winner never considers what the loser discusses. Campaigns boil down to carefully drawn districts, spending more money than one's opponent does, and blasting negative advertisements to catch the public's attention. After the election cycle and with the incumbents safely reelected, legislating turns into an endless stalemate over any roughly contentious national policy. Special interests dominate the process and nitpick exclusions. Legislators run roughshod over any public interest to gather pork-barrel projects for their districts and states. Is there any doubt why Americans are cynical about their national government and institutions? Is there any reason why Americans should trust their elected officials and view government with less contempt? If the Democratic President displays a bankrupt morality through his sexual conduct with a White House intern, should a Republican Senator, who had an extra-marital affair that produced a child, be the one to question his character? In this age of nefarious, self-aggrandizing, partisan politics, it is either symbolic or instructive that *Hustler* publisher Larry Flynt has pushed himself to the forefront of the Clinton scandal. Symbolic for some who worry, and rightfully so, about America's direction. Instructive for others that Flynt's money levels the accusatory political playing field in his chase for duplicitous Clinton attackers.

As part of America's governing elite's message to its people, both the Right and the Left claim—although much more from the Right—that the solution to our social and political problems is a more vibrant civic culture. America has always been based on the active involvement of its people in all social affairs. Our democracy is based on the rule of the people, and Americans are best characterized as joiners who routinely and without hesitation group with others to solve any immediate concern. We are an active lot, motivated by pragmatic concern to help ourselves by getting involved. In fact, our penchant to join together displays our fundamental love of our democratic freedom. But, today our social and political ills reflect a decrease in our civic health. We go to the polls less than any other similarly advanced Western democracy. We hold few judgments on national issues, and distrust with great cynicism politics in general. Americans simply do not get together as they once did, and thus our problems are the result of our lack of cohesiveness.

This work analyzes America's civic virtue and its civic health debate. It seems, as usual I should add, that what we hear from above is not what occurs among us. The answer that a vigorous civic life will restore America's neighborhoods and communities is validated by what is occurring in America's neighborhoods and communities. There, America's civic life proceeds as it has since our country's inception. I argue, then, that America's civic virtue and our associational natures do not lay dormant. In this time of relativized rights, rampant individualism, and market consumerism, we still display interest and concern for our neighbors, schools, and social surroundings. Today, though, our civic virtue proceeds in a variety of forms, many different from the days the pundits herald as some idealistic benchmark. The social changes that create new living arrangements in the family, in the neighborhood, and for the individual, demand a change in how we assess civic life. Instead of this change, the initiators of America's civic virtue debate look to the past to reestablish, reinvent, or return to what can only be called a lost time. Rather than accepting the uncertain present and its mixed results, often this recall of a lost time inhibits the American ability to coalesce to solve our present and mutual concerns.

These are watershed years not only in America but also throughout the world. Technology creates new modes of communication and offers greater access to information. Associated jobs demand wholly new job skills and create unimagined opportunities. While once an industrial behemoth with an inventory of consumer goods, America today adds an expertise in the development of high technology to compete in the global marketplace. While once solely steel and cars, now computer information directs our economy. Yet, in this time of opportunity, growth, and abundant change, today's civic virtue debate focuses almost exclusively on a time when society was simpler, more sedate, and certainly less changeable. In fact, this thinking permeates more than just the political platforms of elected officials. Today's movies, such as *Saving Private Ryan*, throw us back to those days of national unity and character building. Tom Wolfe's *A Man in Full* condemns today's preoccupation for status and its materialistic mania as Wolfe heralds the need for character. It is as if we recognize and cope with the increasing speed of change, but we remain uncomfortable with it. We sense an increasing loss of control and seek a time when control seemed possible. As the 1990s turn to a new millennium, we are enamored with the 1950s. As we grow from the so-called greediness of the 1980s, we level our disgust at the changes wrought by the 1960s. At the turn of the century, we reap the evils of selfish individualism and civic decline from the seeds of counter-culture politics sowed thirty years prior.

Invoking the benefits of the past augments our anxiety about America's present and future. Other films offer this message. *Pleasantville*, for instance, and, to a lesser extent *The Truman Show*, challenge us to assess today's uncertainties against yesterday's rarely acknowledged problems. The 1950s were filled with racial divisions, with a more defined hierarchy in the family and in society, and with fewer opportunities for minorities and women. Today's message must be that uncertainty comes with freedom, and, as Jim Carrey chooses in *The Truman Show*, fulfillment comes from a measure of unpredictability. America needs not an old calculus for the unpredictable or unintended effects of today's freedom. Or, if America does need to embrace an older, traditional calculus, we locate and demonstrate our freedom through our civic associations and our examples of community action. On the whole, however, today's civic virtue debate calls attention to an important problem, infuses it with popular anxiety, and solves it with an impossible return to a time long gone. This outcome can only produce more anxiety, and the cycle of fueling anxiety by promising unrealistic, if not anti-democratic, social changes disillusions society and misdirects our public interest and actions.

While it will be clear what my views are on this national discussion of civic virtue and who misdirects this debate away from causes and solutions to its mere symptoms, a more elemental issue emanates from this work. It is the simple point that today's social ills and the civic virtue solution are far more complex than today's discussion offers. Today's society does confront profound changes that foster worsening conditions for many Americans. In turn, the idea of civic virtue necessitates concerted effort. Instead, what we have is more political posturing than analytical study. First, then, we need more information and less ideological statements from our leaders, both from elected governmental leaders and from corporate leaders. Or, realizing this as fruitless, Americans themselves need to actively take control of the debate and its possible solutions. Fortunately, despite what our leaders tell us, Americans do just this. It is my argument, then, that citizens display civic virtue and demonstrate their democratic abilities on a daily basis in communities across the country. Thus, while told what we lack, we work toward that which we cherish.

However, this work advocates anything but a rose-colored complacency. My message is not simply that what you hear and read from national leaders, social critics, or the media as a whole misleads you. It is that while civic life may be vibrant at the local level, it is most assuredly under-funded and exists against the longest odds. My concept of civic differentiation demarcates the widely-divergent types of civic activity, from the affluent suburban Columbine High School in Littleton, Colorado, to the marginalized, inner-city outpost with only a deteriorating church as a hospitable refuge from violence. Both demonstrate civic action, but both exist at opposite ends of the civic continuum. Resources are abundant with Littleton's surging economy, and thus opportunities, programs, and services are readily accessible. Contrast Colorado's abundant resources with a less dramatic example than the inner-city ghetto. In six weeks after the Columbine shootings, 5 million dollars had been raised for victims, an amount that dwarfs all the money raised in all the other recent high school shootings, from Pearl, Mississippi, to West Paducah, Kentucky, to Jonesboro, Arkansas. Such sums reveal that civic activity benefits from a number of variables other than mere citizen interest and action. Just as with education and health care, inequalities fuel civic disparities.

In short, this notion of civic differentiation and my focus on economic and social inequalities offset my Pollyannish inclinations. After the Columbine shootings, social commentators were quick to conclude that even in the subdued setting of middle-class America, violence and moral decay eats at social institutions. More often than not, the refrain was "if it can happen here, it can happen anywhere," followed by local leaders declaring "this community will come together to heal these wounds." As an alternative to this consensus, as chapter four discusses, it is possible to view Columbine not as an example of random violence. Rather, this latest high school rampage is witness to a mind-numbing culture of anonymity, placelessness, and the loss of identity. The Right and the Left agree that building community—in a sense building an identity and reducing the scale of modern life—is an antidote to our malaise, but most often remedies embrace times past and traditions long since declared discriminatory, biased, and now illegal. The suburbanization of America provides a measure of wealth, of comfort, and of leisure unimagined just a half century ago. It also promotes a kind of individualism that distances us, if we allow it, from our collective responsibilities.

In the end, America today confronts its perpetual problem, most clearly enunciated by Tocqueville in the 1830s: Habits form in freedom that may one day become fatal to that freedom. This means individualism and freedom by themselves do not sustain the society which grants their acceptance and use. In fact, by definitions, individualism is singular, society is plural. Today, in repetition of age-old debates over democratic rule, we attempt to bridge these fundamental discrepancies, sometimes with veiled moralizing, sometimes with moments of success, and most often with unforeseen problems. Political theorists from Aristotle through Adam Smith and the drafters of the U.S. Constitution to today's communitarians have always recognized the tenuous balance between individual liberty and social commitments. Only with episodes such as Columbine does society in unison grasp the inherent difficulty of balancing freedom with collective responsibility.

Also, as the Columbine shootings further underscore, solutions involve economic changes but are not solely economic in nature. A host of social forces, those forces that encourage conservative declarations of a decaying social morality, work for us and work against us simultaneously. Costs come with suburbanization; costs also come with the equality espoused by bureaucracy and routinized administration. However, with my father as my first example, our most certain and effective civic response is, quite simply, to work—as Americans have always worked—by associating to shape, influence, and grapple with the conditions which shape, influence, and grapple with us. Certainly, group action also needs government support and funding, and at times government direction. Most importantly, though, this work of joining has become even more essential for we now grant social acceptance, even social status, to the inequalities that allow us to partition ourselves from each other. America's principal challenge today is how we choose to balance our liberties with our duties and responsibilities to each other. My concern is that our choices reflect both a healthy respect for the traditions that appeal to many with the growing pains of social change that encourage inclusion and a more thoroughly thought-out, digested, and socially articulated sense of equality. It is through my father's actions in our small hometown, then, that Tocqueville's associational life is portrayed most aptly. His service epitomizes what is both elemental and effective in a democratic society, and communities throughout America duplicate similar reservoirs of collective action and social interest. Thus, America does not lack a sense of community and responsibility, it merely needs to wade through the weeds of modernity, stifling inequalities, and contemporary rhetoric to recognize the sturdy shoots of reserve and resolve in groups, towns, and cities throughout the country.

Acknowledgments

As is true at the start of many civic projects, this work had no institutional support. No university or research position existed. No graduate students or secretaries spent their time and energy here. No office technology assisted. No stipends or funding sources helped. However, I mention what did not happen to expose how this work is different than most research projects, and how it is similar to many civic initiatives. Although I had no assistance from any institutional source in the writing and researching of this work, other than the support of Praeger Publishers, I have benefited from the support and encouragement of many friends. I hope, then, that this book works as a bonding mechanism, as an example of how social interaction, however small and mundane, builds lasting connections.

James Sabin of Praeger Publishers was an early and enthusiastic supporter of this project. I hesitated to send Praeger the initial proposal, but I had a quick response telling me to get to work. Sabin is responsible for moving this project forward. Also, thanks to Lynn Zelem, senior production editor, and Kristen Gould, who copyedited the manuscript, often clarifying my jumbled ideas and dense writing style.

Any project of any size and time demands strong friendships. I have had the pleasure of friends interested in the intellectual discussion and in my well-being. Scott Lowry works in parallel fashion through Medieval literature. Megan Edmunds is both an old and a new source of inspiration, as she encourages a refreshing perspective toward civic virtue and political theory. Also, Ray and Shannon Browning, Elke Schaumberg and Charlie Harper, Vicki and Brian Hunter, and Mary Gorman and Paul Fuller all contributed to my writing by first looking after my health.

I am in great debt to Kathi Cowgill. I spent more time writing than tending to our friendship. No person can be as fortunate as I to have such a forgiving, appreciative soul. Similar thoughts apply to Randy Winn. For over a decade now, he has always had a kind word and an even better sense of humor to fend off my more distressing thoughts.

My brother Brad and his wife Stephanie, along with my sister Allison and her husband Kris Athey, put up with my lack of contact for weeks on end. They called, stopped by, and offered good conversation and the love of their children so I could remain close to my family.

I had more support than I deserve from Jen Nelson. She reviewed chunks of this work, always had a sympathetic ear, and provided endless diversions to refresh my attitude. This work benefits from her intelligence and experience, and I benefit from her company.

1

⁓

Our Civic Ideal and Today's Debate

It was a Saturday morning in the summer, 1982, and I was holed up in the basement of the defunct Kallet Theater covered in soot. Home from college, I had on my most worn and dirtied work clothes—long blue jeans and a heavy, cotton, long-sleeved shirt. I had a painter's mask closed tightly around my mouth and nose, but I could still feel the airborne dust I kicked up soaking into my skin and coating my eyelashes. I was in that basement sweeping up inches of dirt, rust, soot, and other unwanted debris. I was working with Russell Charleston, and we had no lighting other than the temporary rigging we snaked in with extension cords from some outside, and at the moment, quite distant place. In fact, it was an archeological excavation, and we were not so carefully ridding the area of the mounds and layers of detritus that had surrounded the identification and cleaning of our main goal: the theater's boiler.

I was in that unlighted, rank basement because of my Dad's civic kindness. Assessing the theater's heating system was one of the first steps in gauging the condition of one of my hometown's landmarks. My father was an electrical contractor, and I was the last of five sons who spent summers in high school, college, and beyond helping the family business. In hindsight, I am certain every job that I was a part of included work well beyond my Dad's stated job description of electrical troubleshooting and construction. Most jobs included what I was doing in that basement. It was grunt work, behind the scenes and unrecognized in the project's biggest picture. I was there because I was an employee, a son, and another pair of hands, but my Dad was there because he was refurbishing one of the town's historic buildings.

He told me how the theater would look three months down the road, and how it would draw people back to downtown. With its thousands of pulsating bulbs, its retiled foyer, and its polished wood flooring in the central ballroom, the Kallet Theater would become a site for big-band dances, Friday night roller-skating, youth theater programs, city forums, antique sales, cooking demonstrations, and other civic functions. Although the theater could no longer compete with the chain movie complexes out on the main commercial drag, it could appeal to many age groups with its historic air and luxurious, although not exactly modern, accommodations. Smack dab in the center of town, perhaps it could help bring a modicum of business to the tired city's center. The town needed a lift, the Kallet sat dormant for too long, and my Dad displayed the civic initiative to revitalize a small part of the city where he and my Mom raised six kids.

But the Kallet Theater project reveals more than just one person's civic commitment. The city had purchased the site and the mayor inquired to some friends about its potential use. These friends, Cal and Cornie Brewster, owned a local insurance business and asked my Dad to investigate the building's physical structure and internal workings. When my Dad reported its fair shape, the Brewsters rounded up interested locals to form a committee. In addition to the Brewsters and my father, Dr. Richard Myers, Shirley and Dave Cockrell, Chris Bourns, Helene Brewer, and Cathy Walton comprised the first board of directors. The Kallet family gave $30,000 to help with repairs. Cathy Walton secured a $43,000 grant to repair the roof. A local heating and plumbing business fixed the heating equipment. Over the years, school classes, Boy Scouts, Brownies, and all sorts of business people and local citizens volunteered time to clean up downtown's signature site.[1]

My Dad's and the others' civic actions exemplify what Alexis de Tocqueville described as the quintessential uniqueness of American society and why, despite democracy's many pitfalls, the American experiment had the ability to overcome its obstacles. Tocqueville writes "In democratic countries knowledge of how to combine is the mother of all other forms of knowledge; on its progress depends that of all others . . .[2] [and] Americans of all ages, all stations in life, and all types of disposition are forever forming associations. . . . In every case, at the head of any new undertaking, where in France you would find the government or in England some territorial magnate, in the United States you are sure to find an association."[3] My father's actions, then, represent how America fulfills its democratic promise: through citizen awareness and initiative and through an intricate and established network of alliances and information, most notably working on local and regional issues. But the media reports that examples such as my Dad's have diminished in contemporary society and politics. Given the growing cynicism and political apathy of the American public, today's social commentary cries out that America's civic life has nearly evaporated.

Contrast my Dad's behavior with what we accept today as our civic behavior. At the national level, the 1996 presidential election displayed nearly record-levels of voter apathy with only 49.6 percent of the eligible electorate participating. Coming on the heels of third party candidate Ross Perot's 19 percent voter showing in 1992, people are either disgusted by major party politics, perceiving neither as a lesser evil, or they simply abstain from political activity altogether. Off-presidential year elections for senators and representatives are even more abysmal, and those voters who do participate represent an ever more biased electorate who are in favor of certain classes, races, and who have certain educational backgrounds. E.J. Dionne claims that "Americans hate politics" because of the false polarization between liberalism and conservatism. To Dionne, neither side has progressed from the 1960s, and both sides fight each other over inane cultural wars. As liberals worry about market rapaciousness but enjoy unrestrained cultural and sexual choices, conservatives focus on morals and virtues but refrain from any economic restrictions. In the end, society, which Dionne views as "not necessarily [a] contradictory mix of liberal instincts and conservative values," is ready for its leaders to progress but cannot get its representatives to disown these easy political targets.[4] In turn, Americans have become decidedly more cynical in response to these activities. While cynicism is destructive to the creation of the trust and commitment necessary to build civic ties and strong communities, cynicism is viewed alternatively as the logical reaction to a politics steeped in a democratic tradition. Jean L. Cohen reports that "Claude Offe has recently argued, unconstrained critical discourse in the public sphere . . . is the form of institutionalized 'distrust' that is actually crucial to maintaining trust and belief in legitimacy—in constitutional democracies."[5] A good bit of cynicism, then, may be a sign of a healthy democracy. The question is, when does cynicism stop drawing us into public debate and start isolating us from our civic ties?

At the local level, where the essence of civic life lies, our civic health and political participation is a mixed bag at best. Citizens can and do develop interest in their communities' growth and well-being, especially when it comes to taxes, but generally most of us do not involve ourselves with overtly political issues. Most follow our children's schooling, many help at church functions or at the health club on occasion, and some even volunteer at the senior center or the local library, but we do not characterize these activities as political or "charged" with meaning. David Mathews reports that "when they see the possibility of working with others to solve problems that concern them, many Americans—including those who disdain formal politics—volunteer for a variety of activities. . . . Citizens, however, will not call what they do in these public activities 'politics.'"[6] Most of the time, people work to pay bills and buy some of life's luxuries, or people save for an upcoming vacation, for the kids' education, or for some long-term investment. Even local issues may seem beyond the humdrum of the daily toil, and thus outside the purview of making ends meet.

Is this then how Americans behave politically? Politics has been professionalized and institutionalized, thus separating the average citizen ever farther from daily involvement. When an issue has immediate and personal effects, people respond quickly and with great skill. But the general idea is that politics has little influence on one's personal life. The public, though, watches, listens, and acts, sometimes above and beyond these research generalizations. The examples of citizen initiatives in the face of long odds and overwhelming institutional barriers, are both breathless and endless. William Greider reports:

In Brooklyn, people first came together in 1978 as East Brooklyn Congregations, sponsored by Catholic and Protestant churches, a synagogue and two homeowners' associations. . . . Their Nehemiah project has built two thousand moderately priced houses in Brooklyn. Their accumulated political clout arranged a patchwork of public and private financing that provided low monthly mortgage payments for the buyers. In Southern California, three allied organizations turned out seven thousand people to lobby Sacramento in a successful campaign to push up the state's minimum wage. In Texas, a statewide network of ten such organizations has won state legislation for health care for the indigent and $100 million in financing to build sewer and water systems for impoverished migrant-worker settlements in the Rio Grande Valley. In Baltimore, a citizens' organization called BUILD (Baltimoreans United in Leadership Development) canvassed neighborhoods on their political priorities and drafted its own agenda for the city—education, housing, jobs—then collected endorsements from seventy thousand citizens.[7]

Finding more examples does not take much digging. In my own backyard, at nearly every public event or public place, petitioners sought citizens' signatures to put a handful of issues, from the sale of water rights to the Denver Broncos' new stadium, on the 1998 November ballot. This allowed the people of the state to decide, rather than the state legislature.

In terms of public sentiment, the media and the resulting popular opinion that Tocqueville fretted over have offered a rather one-sided perspective. Over the last several years all the various media reported on America's declining civic life. David Broder reviews two recent reports, one from the National Committee for Civic Renewal co-chaired by William Bennett and Sam Nunn, the other from the National Issues Forum conducted by John Doble Research Associates. Broder concludes that both studies call for the same remedy: civic revitalization begins when citizens take a greater role than they presently do in the decisions that affect their communities.[8] Over the last several years, our alleged growing inability or disinclination to associate with each other has captured the imaginations of all sorts of social pundits. Harvard's Robert Putnam is the most prominent of the recent initiators of this foment. He applies James Coleman's concept of "social capital"—defined as the social reservoir of trust, norms, and networks that help create common bonds and collective actions—and argues that those beliefs, customs, and associations that "make democracy work" are in decline in America.[9] As Putnam himself would admit, decline does not mean extinction, and other commentators are quick to point out America's strong and constant religious faith and participation are unparalleled by any other industrial nation. Also, some simply believe America's associational life has shifted from the Elks, Lions, Moose, Jaycees, and Chamber of Commerce meetings to kids' soccer, neighborhood watches, community development initiatives, and MADD. Thus, while thoughtful pieces have challenged Putnam's general claim that America's civic vitality, this vibrant interactive glue that molds our political and social activity, has diminished precipitously, the trend has been that the media tacitly accepts this explanation and reiterates Putnam's argument.

Such pervasive recognition, if only meant as an acknowledgment of one possible theory, seeps into public thought and action. In turn, what once was an academic dialogue applying, with caution, Putnam's in-depth study of northern versus southern Italian democratic traditions to the tangential American case, becomes, through mere repetition, an anointed gospel with its own cadre of preachers. It is precisely this seeping sense of fact by re-iteration, and thus growing public accommodation, that disturbed Tocqueville. He wrote that America must guard against the power of majority opinion to squelch differences and diversity. Tocqueville states that "thought is an invisible power and one almost impossible to lay hands on, which makes sport of all tyrannies. . . . I know of no country in which, speaking generally, there is less independence of mind and true freedom of discussion than in America."[10] Ironically, though, Tocqueville has become the touchstone of our civic decline debate. From his insights that strong civic associations tempered the effects of rapacious individualism and the possible growth of a centralized, administrative state, today many champion his ideas as the necessary course for reestablishing stronger social bonds between citizens. With his thoughts in mind, then, my agenda is to open discussion to the topic of our civic life. Given America's otherwise distrustful, cynical, or perhaps simply cautious approach to power and government, the mere reiteration of Tocqueville's ideas with a cursory review of some societal ills has meant that civic erosion has become the accepted parlance.

However, while Putnam raises interesting questions, and this debate has sparked wide-ranging responses from nearly all academic disciplines, the debate itself has become suffocated by political motivations. The sad result is that a perceptive, broad debate that clearly applies to all facets of contemporary American culture is being simplified, if not bastardized, to satisfy political agendas. The political vultures pick at the civic decline thesis to meet their biased machinations. Clearly, a decline in civic life rocks the political Left onto its heels. If it is true that Americans do not clamor together and find their collective voice through their mutual interaction as they once did—in when, the halcyon 1950s?—then the bureaucratic (welfare) state and the disintegration of the nuclear family (feminism and working mothers) are two of the most obvious culprits for political conservatives. What are two of the most prominent social and political trends of the 1990s? One is the growth and political power within the Republican Party of the Christian Right, which wrested control of the House of Representatives from the Democrats for the first time in over forty years. The second is the burbling up of groups like the Promise Keepers, a male-empowerment group which emphasizes a traditional hierarchy within the family, and, in turn, perpetuates an ongoing backlash against women's equality. Because the bureaucratic, overgrown state and the politics of individual freedoms through the social movements of the 1960s and 1970s are typically linked to the Democratic Party, its members are hard-pressed these days to justify any discussion of governmental action for any issue. The noble myth is that we are now paying for our freedoms gained a generation ago when those social movements brought attention to many profound inequities. Perhaps one Left response, the communitarian emphasis on embedded social action and ties, begins to respond to the charges of civic dysfunction. However, while it de-emphasizes the sanctity of individualism, it begins its approach by also accepting the allegations of civic decline.[11]

If the Left rocks backward, the Right has rolled forward applying the lexicon of civic trouble. William Bennett, the former education secretary during the Reagan presidency, holds civic decline as the cause for moral decline and our general loss of virtue. His latest report, *A Nation of Spectators*, co-chaired with the former Democratic Senator Sam Nunn, cites many contemporary ills, to give it an air of bipartisanship, as evidence of our civic disengagement.[12] Our lack of political participation, atrocious public education system, disintegrating families, and out-of-wedlock births are signs that Americans lack the social behavior and moral attitudes that once guided this country. Interestingly, Bennett and Nunn cite numerous current trends and examples of exactly the kind of behavior they believe Americans now lack. It seems the only news in their eyes is bad news.

Also, while Bennett and Nunn call for better families, better schools, and more commitment and political action, they implicate the media for lacking the drive to report on civic and community issues. For the Right, the "liberal" media will always remain a nemesis; ironic in this case because the media has signed on to the civic decline message. To criticize the media keeps the news gathering, reporting, and editorial stands in a self-reflective mood and keeps the conservative message on the offensive for the battle over public opinion. However, the demons Bennett and Nunn cite are symptoms of larger American problems these authors are unwilling to address. The more fundamental concerns are reflective not of a declining civic life in this country, but rather a declining quality of life for far too many Americans. If we need to chastise the media at all, and we do need to do so, it is for echoing Bennett's ideological missives as much as belaboring its lack of civic reporting. As any concerned citizen knows, an engaged society does not need leadership from the media. The media serves to observe and report, not, as Bennett proposes, to lead and perhaps dictate. Bennett sees the media as another institution to be controlled. Tocqueville viewed free newspapers as a source of diverse and vital information for the populace.

In general, much of this debate over civic life undermines its own mission. It divides rather than unites Americans. The Christian Right and its Republican backers deserve much blame for this divisive language, but if these attitudes have seeped into popular opinion, as I believe they have, then society deserves some blame. But society deserves blame only for its knee-jerk belief in this agenda, if accepted without thought. While the Christian Right and conservative Republicans call for civic revival through traditional notions of family, church, and community, I do not question why people latch on to such opinions. These institutions provide the basis for an active politics, especially at the local level. Today, though, a politics of fear supports the case for civic decline and the call for a return to these American foundations. And the undercurrent to this politics is a twisted morality play. James A. Morone captures the political process of our national moral crusade when he states:

> (contemporary moralists) have constructed a simple story. Most Americans are good, but we are surrounded by rampant immorality. The effect of all this sermonizing is to construct an often shadowy, immoral "other." The political result is a great division: a virtuous us, a vicious them. . . . Creating divisions between us and them assuages the many, and if we remember Tocqueville's dictum, it allows the self-righteous majority opinion to "punish" the few evil members of its society. By differentiating society into stereotypes, politics becomes a forum to establish a specific agenda that disregards the interests of the disadvantaged minority.[13]

However, this initial perspective cannot explain, with nuance and insight, the complexity of this fundamental issue. To blame specific conservative religious and political leaders just does not capture the extent of the debate. To implicate society at large for latching onto homilies does a disservice to the activity and the variety that best characterizes American culture. Of course, a specific and, in my view, divisive agenda adds only confusion and hostility to what I see as our misguided national debate. If it is a misguided, ill-defined, poorly discussed, and politically motivated debate, then clarity and tempered solutions are first on my agenda. The changes necessary, though, bring us to the core of what it is to be an American, and to be an individual in America. The debate today offers only a revision to an apparent high-water mark in American society. As Michael Schudson states, "Any notion of 'decline' has to take for granted some often arbitrary baseline. Putnam's baseline is the 1940s and 1950s when the 'long civic generation' . . . came into its own. But this generation shared the powerful and unusual experience of four years of national military mobilization on behalf of what nearly everyone came to accept as a good cause. If Putnam has selected, say, the 1920s as a baseline, would he have given us a similar picture of decline?"[14]

Civic life has become our national discussion because it involves our basic character and how we choose to live with each other. After social scientists analyze the data, after they provide an explanation and others question their ideas, after the media weighs in and popular opinion forms, some rather basic questions about individual action and group dynamics offer themselves for our digestion. William A. Galston gets to these fundamental ideas when he states, "In the end, the least tangible cause of our civic decline—cultural change—may prove to be the most important. Our dominant norms are choice at the level of individual conduct and entitlement in the construction of social policy. But civil society rests on the very different norm of reciprocity: honoring mutual obligations, doing one's fair share, discharging the responsibilities that sustain a system of rights. Are we prepared to accept restraints on choice and entitlement to create a society that can endure?"[15] Our national debate concerning our civic life is a consideration, it seems, of our social contract. It is a momentous time for reflecting on what values are most important and how to implement those values. In essence, this debate is our social and political legacy for future generations.

ADDING SUBTLETY TO OUR CIVIC DISCUSSION

Before I attempt to answer Galston's question, it is important to give this debate an informed subtlety. For Schudson's and Galston's questions point to the complexity of our current social interaction. American society apparently has arrived at a watershed when its citizens and leaders are highly critical of its individual and collective behavior. In a sense we are critical of who we have become. Most often, though, and this is why I rail against the simplicity of the divisive morality play, we create opponents and enemies to deflect our critical self-examination. Again, creating opponents allows for easy answers to our social condition. Having enemies also provides consensus. And consensus is what we lack today.

More importantly, and why it is difficult to see American society changing drastically, we have a history of wringing our hands over our increasingly selfish, materialistic, and individualistic culture. Yet, since individualism, viewed today—and mistakenly so—as connected with ultimate individual freedom, is perhaps the most pervasive constituent of American ideology, our hand wringing leads to little action. We fret over the effects of individualism, just as Tocqueville did when he wrote that "not only does democracy make men forget their ancestors, but also clouds their view of their descendants and isolates them from their contemporaries. Each man is forever thrown back on himself alone, and there is danger that he may be shut up in the solitude of his own heart."[16] Today the civic decline argument states flatly that people are unwilling to give to their communities. They do act alone, in solitude from neighbors and local issues. In their report, Bennett and Nunn argue that everyone needs to join at least one local community issue group and give their time and energy to some public project. Sound advice, and the Christian Right and conservative agenda deserves attention because it does offer sources for connecting citizens. Their views are appealing because they contain legitimate resources and avenues to attack civic concerns, and while I continue to criticize their overall simplicity, their ideas hold seeds for a growing civic society. Yet, while some of their seeds are productive, others are at best barren, and still others strangle openness, acceptance, and tolerance.

While American society has responded in the past with dramatic change—Progressive Era reforms—our hand wringing has not moderated our increasing individualism. Barry Alan Shain notes, "It was not until aggressive nationalist public policies were adopted, after both America's entry into World War II and later the implementation of prominent Supreme Court decisions of the 1950s through the 1970s, that the individualist ethical vision and its adherents finally succeeded in supplanting the popular but often intolerant communalist ethical tradition."[17] Ironically, then, while generating popular concern, our growing individualism benefits millions of Americans previously subjected to social and legal barriers—the very obstacles Tocqueville saw in the power of majority opinion. In essence, we have traded social and political unity and consensus for greater individual freedoms and equality. And while these gains appear to uphold basic freedoms, for instance the civil rights movement, the women's movement, and consumer activism, public debate also notes that these advances are at times limited to legal channels and are not wholly accepted in American thought. Individualism appears as a double-edged sword. While we worry about its effects, it also benefits many. While it satisfies the American belief in independence and initiative, it also detracts from our sense of belonging and commitment to each other. Since the question of our double-edged individualism is a key component of our civic debate, a similar complexity exists for understanding our civic life.

For Tocqueville, individualism was a new social condition. It germinates from the growth of democracy and yet undermines that very political condition. He states, "Individualism is a calm and considered feeling which disposes each citizen to isolate himself from the mass of his fellows and withdraw into the circle of family and friends; with this little society formed to his taste, he gladly leaves the greater society to take care of itself . . . [and while] egoism sterilizes the seeds of every virtue; individualism at first only dams the spring of public virtues, but in the long run it attacks and destroys all the others too and finally merges into egoism."[18] Tocqueville argues, however, that America had resolved the isolationist route of individualism with a compelling counterweight. He believed that the strong, vibrant associational life America displayed worked to offset individualism's negative effects. In a sense, America had a refined, informed view of self-interest. For Tocqueville describes these actions as:

The doctrine of self-interest properly understood . . . [and] it is among the Americans of our time that it has come to be universally accepted. It has become popular.

One finds it at that root of all actions. It is interwoven in all they say. You hear it as much from the poor as from the rich. . . . The doctrine of self-interest properly understood does not inspire great sacrifices, but every day it prompts some small ones; by itself it cannot make a man virtuous, but its discipline shapes a lot of orderly, temperate, moderate, careful, and self-controlled citizens. If it does not lead the will directly to virtue, it establishes habits which unconsciously turn it that way.[19]

Today's social commentators argue that our self-interest is wrongly understood as "negative" freedom—the freedom to act as Tocqueville's isolationist individual and pursue activities, lifestyles, and public policies that detract from our collective character. Self-interest wrongly understood pursues selfish gain without the ability to control its effects. It undermines our associational life, and in turn calls democracy into question. This is the power of contemporary moralists' claims. Through Tocqueville's sophisticated understanding of individualism, recognizing its inherent dangers as well as its benefits, they state our expression of individualism has jumped from productive and rightly understood to debilitating and socially-defective.

The crux of noting the double-edged results of the growth of our individualistic culture—in that individual gains have compromised some collective identity—is that any call for a return to a time of supposed greater civic life often calls for a return to a culture without these recent hard-won freedoms. In fact, any use of the prefix "re" as in *return, recreating*, and *rebuilding*, neglects the advances of the last thirty-five years. To create a civic culture today, we need to accept the changes of the last two generations and incorporate those cultural characteristics into our plans. To simply return to some determined benchmark—and who determines the benchmark?—misses the effects of cultural change, whether positive or not.

Some remedies offered to renew our civic life look to a time in the past when society was not just different, but unique, as Schudson notes, because we had consensus from a world war, familiarity with a powerful president, and a post-war defined enemy. Do we need another cold war with an obvious external enemy? Terrorists and certain other religions and regions of the world are filling in nicely. Do we want to obliterate all the social and legal gains of the last thirty to forty years to achieve a greater sense of civic solidarity? Some I have criticized above give indications that gains for minorities and especially women have led to our present malaise. The last generation has seen the rise of identity politics, where well-defined groups successfully organize and push their particular interests through the legislative arena. Why is this such a common practice and one that produces such rancor? Because established institutional channels traditionally block these groups' search for equal rights and recognition. The exponential rise in pressure groups and their resort to a "juridical model of politics" exist because conventional politics responds most actively to organized interests rather than to the unorganized or to specific individuals.[20]

How can greater equality for all citizens have a profoundly negative effect on society as a whole? The answer is that in an open, democratic society, it cannot. But many argue—religious groups, moralists, conservatives—that the rights granted to homosexuals, the gains of the women's movement, and other social conditions like drug use and teen pregnancy have led to a permissiveness in society, a society where "anything goes." In fact, these social commentators argue that Tocqueville cited growing equality as one of democracy's most serious concerns. However, his caution was directed at how social equality—that is, a growing equality of circumstances in comparison to aristocratic Europe—would hinder political liberty as the equality between citizens produces a majority opinion that restricts the expression of differences. The present argument, though, attempts to stifle the expression, acceptance, and inclusion of differences by referring to an American morality, a Christian heritage, a national legacy, or some other exclusionary theme. Infiltrated by immigrants, corrupted by criminals, and pillaged by the poor, the exclusionary oratories are reactionary attempts to protect the oracles' one vision of life. Instead of viewing these problems as part of their society, they see these differences as "interlopers" who must be contained or punished. As Morone states, "What is lost is the image of shared fate against common troubles. Benedict Anderson writes that the very idea of a nation rests on 'imagined communities'— an idea that people share a common experience, a common fate, and common values. . . . Moral panics erode liberalism itself."[21]

If we seek to remedy today's debilitating individualism and its effects on our social trust and commitment, we need to address topics that the current civic decline debate fails to mention. Beyond the morality play that pits segments of society in fear of and opposition to each other, one initial consideration is to pursue a national dialogue without making accusations. But political points are too easy to score in today's acrimonious, selfish climate. For instance, the last decade has seen a dramatic change in reducing the national government's size and influence in Americans' lives. Given this social sea of change, even Democrats question the ability of government to solve all social issues. Galston states that one fundamental commitment that needs rethinking is that "New Deal-style economic liberals would have to acknowledge that the growth of government isn't always compatible with a strong civil society."[22] Such attitudinal changes come with the high cost of lost power, jobs, and large sums of entrenched money. With these high stakes, reasoned, enlightened public discourse is at a premium. Typically, Americans witness a shouting match of negative commercials that focus on personal failings more than failing issues. We will determine the seriousness with which we approach our civic life by the level of intelligent discourse. Already, as I have noted, conservative interests have monopolized the debate to promote their social and political agendas. This should come as no surprise, though, as they maintain an inordinate amount of power. Thus, they are the most heavily invested in maintaining their influence. Generally speaking, groups like senior citizens, the wealthy, and businesses exercise this power by being some of the most influential political actors.

TOPICS LEFT OUT OF TODAY'S DEBATE

Turning from the noble cry for enlightened discussion to the specific issues of the civic life debate, the first consideration is how we define the debate itself. Putnam creates a rather general categorization of the concept of "social capital," using not just electoral turnout, but also newspaper readership, the amount of voluntary associations, and civic attitudes like law-abidingness, interpersonal trust, and cooperativeness. In turn, we need to broaden our idea of what today constitutes civic life. Schudson argues that, "The concept of politics has broadened enormously in thirty years. Not only is the personal political, . . . but the professional and occupational is also political. A woman physician or accountant can feel that she is doing politics—providing a role model and fighting for recognition of women's equality for men—every time she goes to work. The same is true for African American bank executives or gay and lesbian military officers. . . . The decline of the civic in its conventional forms, then, does not demonstrate the decline of civic-mindedness."[23] While many define associational life by the number and type of civic groups within society, especially as viable counterweights to government, Putnam's challengers mainly attack his accounting of solely traditional groups. Not only are soccer moms a form of associational life, but other under-recognized interaction such as the growth of community college or continuing education courses; the growth of third spaces like coffee shops, bookstores, and restaurants; and the proliferation of all sorts of health, leisure, and informational classes or groups, provides greater insight into the vitality of our civic health.

Theda Skocpol cites additional factors that the civic health debate must note. First, she calls into question the idea that associational life was a spontaneous result of similarly interested citizens. The "romanticized Tocqueville" interpretation, the one that right-wing groups endorse and promulgate, is that these groups sprung up from the average citizen on the street, and only through these citizen group actions do we have a history of successful democratic experiences. Skocpol argues that these citizen initiatives were accompanied by other advantageous actions. She states:

> the American Revolution, and the subsequent organization of competitive national and state elections under the Constitution of 1789, triggered the founding of newspapers and the formation of local and translocal voluntary associations much faster and more extensively than just nascent town formation can explain. The openness of the U.S. Congress and state legislatures to organized petition drives, the remarkable spread of public schooling, and the establishment of U.S. post offices in every little hamlet were also vital enabling factors, grounded in the very institutional core of the early U.S. state.[24]

Skocpol's concern is that state activity interacted with local initiative to create civic life, and any understanding of America's civic health cannot denounce the intrusiveness of government in group formation. Rather, our civic health is in part dependent upon how state and society interact.

Jean L. Cohen takes Skocpol's argument a step further. She believes Putnam's construction of "social capital" and his emphasis on the importance of voluntary associations in determining civic health undervalue a host of other influential and determining relations. She notes that in Putnam's historical account of Northern Italy's civic-mindedness, he refers to these other state-centered variables but in the long run discounts their influence. Yet, it seems necessary for civic health to produce citizen trust in each other and in the state, to have a "professionalized public administration and credible state impartiality in the enforcement of laws . . . strong and autonomous courts, reliable administrative state structures, and confidence that legislative processes and the administration of justice will be impartial. . . ."[25] Civic health is a complex, multi-layered concept dependent upon a host of other influential factors in determining its viability. To ignore these other variables misleads as it simplifies, and this often produces similar misleading and simplistic interpretations of our civic life from our political leaders and our media. Cohen attacks Putnam for a reductionist narrow-mindedness when she argues:

> That voluntary association is *evidence* of social cooperation and trust is both undeniable and almost tautological, but why is it construed as the only significant source of social capital? Why are democratic political institutions, the public sphere,

and law absent from the theory and analysis of how social trust is developed? The answer is obvious: once the state is defined and dismissed as a third-party enforcer, once law is turned into sanctions that provide for a certain level of order but no more, once institutions are dismissed as irrelevant to social trust because their genesis already presupposes social trust, and once a vital civil society is reduced to the presence or absence of intermediate voluntary associations, no other source of social trust is conceivable.[26]

Cohen's statement captures the complexity that the civic life debate deserves. For she augments Putnam's ideas with a richer, more varied interpretation of how civic life spreads and from where it begins. Putnam's ideas seem too simplistic, too mono-casual, and too linear in comparison. Cohen provides the nuance that any adequate discussion over our civic life needs. To state flatly that reducing government's size and influence in American life will create opportunities for greater voluntary associations to flourish, as is the most resonate political spiel over the last decade, points more to political agendas than to reasoned analysis. Such a statement may be valid and supported with many examples, but to ignore the numerous other factors that foster our civic interaction, and more importantly, how we come to understand how we define what civic life means, emasculates the debate, narrows our options, and obviously favors those who establish the agenda for change, or non-change, as our case may be.

A second concern that Skocpol mentions is the generational effects on civic activity. Any sophisticated understanding of our civic life must recognize that the tumultuous 1960s had profound social and political effects on the youngest, most active and agitated segment of society. Skocpol claims "Putnam does not view a 'sixties and seventies period effect' as an important cause of declining civic engagement, on the grounds that everyone would have dropped out in equal numbers. But . . . historical social scientists have hypothesized that epochal watersheds have their biggest influence on the outlooks of young adults. Perhaps Americans reaching adulthood in the sixties and seventies looked anew at the world, and did not find so attractive those civic associations that their elders still held dear."[27] While cautious distrust is sewn into the American character, in fact this distrust typically offers a healthy interaction between the government and its people, the divisions produced by the murder of popular public figures, the Vietnam War, the Watergate conspiracy, continued racial tension, and the many openly hostile social movements pushed this distrust into unbridled anger, rejection, and contempt. Why, given this backdrop, would a young citizen choose to participate in a traditional civic group? How, given that Vietnam veterans comprise up to half the homeless population, could established veterans groups relate to and somehow represent these returning soldiers? Perhaps the more apt question would be, How have these traditional groups survived the upheaval of the 1960s and 1970s, and if there are some that have not survived, are there any new civic groups initiated by this generation that have taken their place?

Finally, the market's role receives scant attention in how it affects our civic health. In comparison to the professionalized campaign process, the well-heeled lobbying efforts, and the inroads to access that money confers, civic associations demand more time and energy than anything else. The argument may be that if a citizen balks at entering state or national politics because of its professionalized, monied interests, local communities provide a tangible civic outlet. No democratic skills or prior experience are necessary. The essential point that nearly all social commentators make, from both the Left and the Right, is to "just do it." But time and energy may be the very commodities that Americans feel in increasingly short supply. Why? As David M. Gordon states, "Over the past twenty years, real hourly take-home pay for production and nonsupervisory workers—representing over 80 percent of all wage-and-salary employees—has declined by more than 10 percent. The economy has grown massively since the mid-1960s, but workers' real spendable wages are no higher now than they were almost thirty years ago."[28] Today, the vast majority of people work more hours for less spendable wages than in the 1960s. If ever a source of contention existed that could spur social change, it is this basic fact.

However, instead of viewing this economic trend as a political issue and rallying around public policies that distribute economic gains and burdens differently, citizens internalize their private troubles and view their own and their neighbors' difficulties as the workings of a inherently just market system. In a sense, they are politically immobilized by their and society's market socialization, especially with the fall of communism and the number of new states turning to market economies. It is the American creed of individualism and freedom to nurture an economy based on supply and demand. It allows consumers to determine what they want, and it fosters competitiveness and industriousness to gain consumer confidence. But Galston notes, just as economic liberals must concede that the growth of government is not always conducive to a strong civil society, "free-market conservatives would have to acknowledge that the operation of the contemporary economy isn't always compatible with a strong civil society. While social capital is place-specific, our corporations give less and less weight to historic community ties. The owner of Malden Mills became an instant national hero when he decided to rebuild his plant after a devastating fire."[29] In this age of globalization, corporations take advantage of their ability to seek the lowest wage rate in order to remain competitive.

The effects of these corporate pullouts devastate communities and further erode civic trust while they place unexpected economic burdens on citizens. The *raison d'être* is corporate survivability, but the communities that remain face the more difficult survival.

Additionally, Morone forcefully argues that today's moralists who use the civic decline thesis to exacerbate fear and animosity between disparate social groups avoid completely the differences that the market economy fosters. He claims the inherent division against the least advantaged is the most disturbing aspect of today's discussion. He argues:

> The celebration of virtue stops at the market's edge. The lamentations about lost values are directed largely at poor people. There is scarcely a word about what the privileged owe their society. American troubles [have been framed by conservatives as caused by the] lazy, self-indulgent, criminal poor [who] are responsible for their own troubles, the growth of liberal welfare government, and the dwindling opportunities for the hard-working, moral us.[30]

What about those hard-working us? Edward N. Wolff reports:

> New research, based on data from federal surveys, shows that between 1983 and 1989 the top 20 percent of wealth holders received 99 percent of the total gain in marketable wealth, while the bottom 80 percent of the population received only 1 percent. America produced a lot of new wealth in the 1980s—indeed, the stock market boomed—but almost none of it filtered down. . . . The most recent data suggest that these trends have continued. My preliminary estimates indicate that between 1989 and 1992, 68 percent of the increase in total household wealth went to the richest 1 percent—an even larger share of wealth gain than between 1983 and 1989 (which was 62%).[31]

After giving these stark numbers, Wolff adds, "Economic worries may be at the root of much of the political anger in America today, but there is almost no public debate about the growth in wealth inequality, much less the steps needed to reverse current trends. The debate needs to start with an understanding of how and why America's pie is getting sliced so unequally."[32]

While the economic trends cause alarm and Americans worry over their diminishing buying power, citizens only hear about moral decay and read about the signs of their corrupt society. Little wonder why citizens believe that government activity has also no effect on their lives—because the news does not report and the politicians do not address what is most on the minds of Americans. Little wonder why citizens choose not to participate in politics or opt not to join civic organizations—because if more and more of their time is spent earning a wage to pay for life's essentials—or dare I say, conveniences—then even the minimal requirements of time and energy come at a premium price. Conversely, who does have the time and energy? Ironically—or is it assuredly?—those whom the present system already benefits, namely the rich. As Verba, Schlozman, and Brady report, "While it is difficult to give time to a campaign without also being expected to give money, the opposite is not true. . . . [Also,] those at the top of the income hierarchy produce more than their proportionate share of votes, campaign hours, contacts, protests, and campaign dollars. . . . Indeed, when it comes to campaign dollars, the top two income groups—who form less than 10 percent of the population—donate more than half of the money."[33] Of course, if the input into the political system is biased in the favor of the few who have the time and money to take part, then the output is skewed in their favor too. These authors ask, "Who enjoys the luxury of money or time to devote, if desired, to political participation? In case it was not apparent before Hemingway's famous observation, the rich have more money. Moreover, in comparison with other developed democracies, income and wealth are distributed relatively unequally in the United States, a trend that has become more pronounced over the past decade and a half."[34] More often than not, these later issues are what dominate the headlines, the news articles, and the television reports. When we do speak about the disadvantaged, we often let our stereotypes speak for us.

Yet, to cast blame toward certain segments of society merely exacerbates existing divisions. Certainly, American society, as presently structured, grants far greater privileges to the wealthy and to corporations than to an ever squeezed and shrinking middle class and below. But to solve our social problems and to create civic initiative and strong communities, we need the work and effort of all members of communities, from corporate citizens and the rich to the most underprivileged. Christopher Lasch castigates the rich for "revolting" against the rest of society by sealing themselves off from moral corruption, educational nightmares, and criminal activity with gated communities and cosmopolitan outlooks. As much as the poor and disadvantaged have no representation in their communities, Lasch explains that the wealthy refrain from participating because they can secure public goods through their private actions. In a cost-effective world, they are above and beyond the communities in which they live.[35]

To better address the debate of our civic health, these factors need to become the primary topics for directing community action and public policy, although today they remain overlooked and underdeveloped. My argument is that the economic health of most Americans has diminished significantly over the last generation, to the point where their principal focus is on their immediate economic concerns. As Greider reports, "Since 1973, wages in real terms, discounted for inflation, have been stagnant or declining. . . . The rewards changed most dramatically in the 1980s—at the very time government was cutting tax burdens for the well-to-do."[36] And with such benefits to the wealthy, it is quite ironic that they are most often strong advocates of reducing government's influence in people's lives. In general, when, or if, civic or political issues capture the public's attention, it is most often related directly to their economic interests. We are becoming a nation of have and have-nots, and economic disparities often lead to the social behavior that produces the moralist's condemnation of a depraved society.

MORE QUESTIONS THAN ANSWERS

The fundamental questions to which today's civic discussion alludes, questions that we may likely neglect, involve how we choose to interact socially and politically. At the broadest level, they focus on the primacy of the individual in contemporary society and the relative power of democratic majorities to control individual behavior. For it seems today's civic decline message is a message about too much freedom and its disastrous consequences. Some conservatives argue our lack of strong communities and decaying moral fabric is due to the freedom associated with a no-fault divorce culture, easy access to abortion, and in general a sense of freedom to choose whatever lifestyle one wants. Although this paints an extreme picture, the civic health debate is a direct response to these perceived dramatic freedoms without associated responsibilities, duties, and moral constraints. At the heart of the debate is how does society commit to and sustain a common vision without squashing the differences and variety essential to a vibrant, multicultural people? Is our fundamental issue whether American society has strayed too far in protecting individual freedoms and rights and promoting diversity, and whether today's call for rights with responsibilities and freedoms with duties is in response to our inability to establish modes of accepted behavior?

Or, if too much diversity and freedom is not our undoing, is there some deeper issue here that needs illumination? For, while conservatives attack the moral decline of our individualistic society, they object when liberals begin to attack the individualistic behavior of corporate America. Suddenly, there can never be too much economic freedom or too much freedom from government interference. Socially, though, individuals must abide by a strict set of Christian beliefs, communally established and directed. Contemporary ills are a product of straying too far from family traditions. The debate has never transferred over to the duties and responsibilities of corporations, primarily because conservatives have directed this debate and because economic freedom is an accepted tenet of America's success. To challenge these ideas, Nicholas Lemann writes:

> With respect to the United States, the opposite of Putnam's theory would be this: There has been relatively little general decline in civic virtue. To the extent that the overall civic health of the nation did deteriorate, the dip was confined to the decade 1965 to 1975—when, for example, crime and divorce rose rapidly—and things have been pretty stable since then. The overwhelming social and moral problem in American life is instead the disastrous condition of poor neighborhoods, almost all of which are in cities. The model of a healthy country and needy ghettos would suggest a program much closer to the 'liberal social policy' from which Putnam wants us to depart. . . . The difficulty with such a program is that it is politically inconvenient. It would involve, by contemporary standards, far too much action on the part of the government, with the benefits too skewed toward blacks. *The model of an entire United States severely distressed in a way that is beyond the power of government to correct is more comforting.*[37]

Lemann's insights point to deeper issues within our civic health debate. While he questions the value of the debate itself, and thus implicates those who are most involved as politically motivated and truly socially unaware, he also calls to task the American fear and rejection of government action and power. Railing against government is an easy, simplistic political move, but as Skocpol noted above, only through the intertwining of government action and local drive did America's virtuous civic culture emerge. Skocpol's ideas also demand that we reassess the casual effects of our civic health debate. While today the usual conception is that our declining civic virtue undermines any sense of maintaining a strong democracy, she offers instead that an energized political democracy, one that creates opportunities for citizens to take part rather than increasingly demanding less of them, could be the impetus to building a stronger civic culture. In either case, Lemann's and Skocpol's alternatives allow us to reveal the limits of our current civic debate: the difficulty in addressing our fundamental national fears, the political message and agenda that underlies the debate, and the inability, given these other obstacles, to adequately assess viable solutions to these problems.

If solutions are politically untenable and socially charged, then the search for answers can come from dispassionate, removed figures. To better grasp the enormity of this debate and the complexity of the basic issues that affect how democracy functions, I employ democratic theorists to address America's uncertain democratic times. Tocqueville's ideas have been confiscated to push the conservative agenda of rebuilding our civic associations to nurture our democratic promise. But Tocqueville's ideas need not be politically-charged. Other political theorists, like Jefferson and Rousseau, offer advice and warnings for democracy's predicaments. I seek answers from several theorists because each offers insight worthy for our times, and because our times are unique and thus I need to draw from several sources. I do not seek solutions based on the unified ideas of one theorist. I seek a patische of relevant ideas and apply them to our civic virtue debate.

Debating democracy's health by invoking relevant theoretical ideas is an academic's summer pastime, and many would question the applicability of this approach. If our civic virtue debate is of utmost social importance, then immediate fixes are in order. For many, to ponder Rousseau's meaning of the general will has little relevance to creating strong families today. If this is the case, I need to combine my penchant for theoretical ideas with practical politics and social interaction, where life is muddled, mixed, and dirtied without concern for uniformity or generalizability. As much as Tocqueville described the American ideal of civic life, his characterization still applies many years later. If nothing else, when confronted with obstacles that affect people personally and / or emotionally, American civic life is as vibrant as ever. But the opportunities to express this civility are being reduced by trends that need dramatic change; trends, such as economic freedom, that have become accepted elements of American freedom, or trends that push citizens away from civic life, such as the influence of money in professionalized politics. As all these theorists argue, democracy flourishes when a rough equality induces civic participation to express freely-chosen interests. I argue that rough equality is nonexistent, and freely-chosen interests are constrained by this inequality. In turn, our civic life disappears and democracy withers because these other conditions are not met.

Today's civic debate glosses over the true causes of civic dysfunction. We simplify its complexity to reduce its inherent difficulty. We often fail to change our own behavior as we live paradoxical lives. We create imaginary enemies to satisfy our search for an easy answer. We latch on to quick fixes, which removes fear and guilt from our own underdeveloped analyses. We rely on others to provide solutions because many problems are seemingly distant and intractable. When we perceive problems that demand our immediate attention, we feel we lack the skills or knowledge to tackle them. Also, we often lack interest in public life because we concentrate on immediate issues, mainly economic and familial ones. We search for intelligent public discourse but believe we get selfish officials with self-serving interests. We hesitate to believe in established institutions and their effectiveness, but we adamantly uphold the values and beliefs that first gave rise to these institutions and to which they serve. These views are difficult to embrace because they call our actions into question, and they are even more difficult to understand how they determine our civic lives. But these are our contradictions, and no less than our democratic health necessitates, we acknowledge and change our behavior in order to change our social, economic, and political condition. Only then will our civic life change. Only then will our civic life become a moot concern.

We need not agonize over our civic life just yet, despite my view of the dichotomy between our beliefs and our actions. If we look away from institutionalized, professionalized politics, a wealth of civic activity captures our attention. I argue that despite the exhortations about our lack of civic virtue, too many examples exist—of citizens engaged in common efforts to press for basic rights and services against established powers—to believe fully that civic life has died. Do I contradict myself, then? On one hand, I cite the duplicity between our words and actions—the contradictions we live that yearn for community and public interaction yet maintain individualistic choices and lifestyles. At times, I state we do not pursue thoroughly reasoned discourse, preferring instead public policies made up of sound bites and political machinations. On the other hand, I give examples of how people today are living up to our Tocquevillean heritage of strong civic ties as the essence of a democratic society. My answer to this apparent contradiction is to give two views of our current condition. To explain our civic unease, Richard Stivers states:

> Morality in the conventional sense of the term has all but disappeared; at the same time a technological and bureaucratic morality has arisen to fill the void. But this latter morality leaves no room for individual ethical decision. . . . In the modern world freedom is closely identified with consumer choice. As a consequence the individual can make genuine ethical decisions at a heavy price—*nonconformity*. We are ensnared in a vicious circle: If ethical action is needed to understand social reality, then the reduced opportunity to make ethical choices leaves us only dimly aware of the ersatz morality that has us in its embrace. . . . The new American morality is in a very real sense an anti-morality. . . . Because of our fascination with technology, . . . we do not perceive the need to limit its growth and expansion into every sphere of human existence. Technology is at bottom nothing more than an expression of power. . . . My thesis is that technical and bureaucratic rules are the "morality" of technology. . . . Both public opinion and visual images serve the interest of technology.[38]

Stivers points out the difficulties we as people and as citizens must confront on a daily basis. We live in a world that creates itself anew seemingly overnight. Single businesses do not crop up anymore; behemoth malls suddenly emerge. The pace of life seems to quicken daily as computerization makes communication around the globe faster and easier, makes workers and whole industries more efficient, makes everyday conveniences seem like luxuries—or should that be, makes today's luxuries seem like everyday conveniences—and even makes movies more fantastic and life-like. As a consequence, our ethics and morals begin to reflect only material, market decisions, thus unable to give meaning and perspective to these changes. Contradictory lives seem a natural consequence if we are beholden to technology's changes.

To contrast Stivers' dire perspective about our inherent difficulties in redressing complex societal changes, and to bolster my argument for civic vitality, Lemann presents an interesting contrast. He writes:

> I have lived in five American cities: New Orleans, Cambridge, Washington, Austin, and Pelham, NY. The two that stand out . . . as the most deficient in the Putnam virtues—the places where people I know tend not to have elaborate hobbies and not to devote their evenings and weekends to neighborhood meetings and activities—are Cambridge and Washington. The reason is . . . work absorbs all energy. It is what people talk about at social events. Community is defined functionally, not spatially: it's a neighborhood peer group rather than a community. . . . To people living this kind of life, many of whom grew up in a bourgeois provincial environment and migrated to one of the capitals, [Putnam's civic decline] theory makes sense, because it seems to describe their own situation so well.[39]

Just as Skocpol notes a generational effect for joining civic groups, Lemann points to several other conditional factors. Perhaps the civic decline message that emanates from our power centers is more a reflection of their particular, jaundiced environment than an accurate portrayal of American social life. Perhaps civic decline can be linked to a specific class, those who opt out of their communal attachments for more private rewards. As Verba, Schlozman, and Brady report, and as Lasch wrote for many years, perhaps the wealthy and the politically ambitious display the most civic absenteeism, and given their powerful social roles, their guilty consciences filter down into popular opinion, although popular action contradicts this growing sentiment.

My answer is that civic life does exist, and because it confronts difficult and changing obstacles, it is also my belief that more participants, ones who see collective action as a path toward successful political change, individual growth, and fulfillment, are necessary. As a society, we are quite a ways off from this condition, but more than enough seeds of action exist to warrant optimism. In response, my work focuses on the validity of the civic decline argument and how economic and social equality would alter the scope and tenor of today's one-sided dialogue. First, we need a good grasp of the debate's issues, and how this one-sided, usually conservative view misguides us with Tocqueville's words and with their view of civic virtue.

NOTES

1. I must note that this is just one example of my father's civic commitments as he was integral to many community projects in my hometown of Oneida, New York, and throughout Central New York. Some of those other projects include being a founding member of Kanon Valley Country Club and the Presbyterian Home in New Hartford, New York. He contributed more than just electrical expertise to the Veteran's Memorial Playfield in Oneida and to Vernon Downs Raceway, a harness-racing track located in Vernon, New York. I would be remiss if I neglected my mother's community service too, as I remember vividly her efforts through the PTA, our local church functions, Brownies and Boy Scouts, and her time spent on the Board of Education.

2. Alexis de Tocqueville, *Democracy in America*, ed. J. P. Mayer (New York: HarperPerennial, 1969), 517.

3. Ibid., 513.

4. E. J. Dionne, *Why Americans Hate Politics* (New York: Simon and Schuster, 1991), 9–14.

5. Jean L. Cohen, "American Civil Society Talk," Institute for Philosophy and Public Policy, (summer 1998), (http://www.puaf.umd.edu/ipp/summer98/), 2.

6. David Mathews, *Politics for the People: Finding a Responsible Public Voice* (Urbana, Ill.: University of Illinois Press, 1994), 121.

7. William Greider, *Who Will Tell the People: The Betrayal of American Democracy* (New York: Simon and Schuster, 1992), 222–223.

8. David S. Broder, "Up From Apathy," *The Washington Post National Weekly Edition* (July 6, 1998): 4.

9. Robert D. Putnam, *Making Democracy Work: Civic Traditions in Modern Italy* (Princeton, N.J.: Princeton University Press, 1993). See also Robert D. Putnam, "Bowling Alone: America's Declining Social Capital," *Journal of Democracy* (January, 1995): 65–78.

10. Alexis de Tocqueville, *Democracy in America*, 254–255.

11. Michael J. Sandel, *Democracy's Discontent: America in Search of a Public Philosophy* (Cambridge, Mass.: The Belknap Press of Harvard University Press, 1996).

12. William Bennett and Sam Nunn, "Turning a Nation of Spectators Into Doers," *Los Angeles Times*, reprinted in *Boulder Daily Camera* (July 12, 1998): 6E.

13. James A. Morone, "The Corrosive Politics of Virtue," *The American Prospect*, no. 26 (May–June 1996): 32.

14. Michael Schudson, "What If Civic Life Didn't Die?" *The American Prospect*, no. 25 (March–April 1996): 18.

15. William A. Galston, "Won't You Be My Neighbor?" *The American Prospect,* no. 26 (May–June 1996): 18.

16. Alexis de Tocqueville, *Democracy in America,* 508.

17. Barry Alan Shain, *The Myth of American Individualism: The Protestant Origins of American Political Thought* (Princeton, N.J.: Princeton University Press, 1994), 323–324.

18. Tocqueville, 506–507.

19. Ibid., 526–527.

20. Jean Bethke Elshtain, *Democracy on Trial* (New York: Basic Books, 1995), 26–27.

21. James A. Morone, "The Corrosive Politics of Virtue," *The American Prospect* 33.

22. William A. Galston, "Won't You Be My Neighbor?" *The American Prospect* 17.

23. Michael Schudson, "What If Civic Life Didn't Die?" *The American Prospect* 18.

24. Theda Skocpol, "Unraveling From Above," *The American Prospect,* no. 25 (March–April 1996): 23.

25. Jean L. Cohen, "American Civil Society Talk," Institute for Philosophy and Public Policy, 3.

26. Ibid.

27. Theda Skocpol, "Unravelling From Above," *The American Prospect* 23.

28. David M. Gordon, *Fat and Mean: The Corporate Squeeze of Working Americans and the Myth of Managerial 'Downsizing'* cited by Jack Beatty, "What Election '96 Should Be About," *The Atlantic Monthly* (May 1996): 114. In Gordon's book, see 16–20 and graph on 19.

29. Galston, "Won't You Be My Neighbor?" 16.

30. Morone, "The Corrosive Politics of Virtue," 33.

31. Edward N. Wolff, "How The Pie Is Sliced," *The American Prospect,* no. 22 (summer 1995): 58.

32. Ibid., 59.

33. Sidney Verba, Kay Lehman Schlozman, and Henry E. Brady, "The Big Tilt: Participatory Inequality in America," *The American Prospect,* no. 32 (May–June 1997): 75, 77.

34. Ibid., 75.

35. Christopher Lasch, *The Revolt of the Elites and the Betrayal of Democracy* (New York: W.W. Norton & Company, 1995): 25–49.

36. William Greider, *Who Will Tell The People,* 86.

37. Nicholas Lemann, "Kicking in Groups," *The Atlantic Monthly* (April 1996): 26.

38. Richard Stivers, *The Culture of Cynicism: American Morality in Decline* (Cambridge, Mass.: Blackwell Publishers, 1994): ix.

39. Nicholas Lemann, 26.

2

‿

The Sham of Civic Virtue

This chapter has two themes. One is that today's civic virtue debate lacks sufficient insight to provide worthwhile public objectives. Instead, it focuses on our moral condition to the exclusion of all other social elements. Thus, it seeks remedies by changing individual behavior while it underestimates the effects political and economic activity have on individual behavior. As a representative example, I examine Gertrude Himmelfarb's recent work describing America's civic condition. The second theme is related to the first, but it starts from a more theoretical background. It questions the application of Tocqueville's views of American society to our current civic health. I offer reservations about his views by way of analyzing what I believe are several myths, both past and present, about American society. Although Tocqueville's views provide intellectual insight for our supposed social evils and to our civic solutions, they also have been crafted by and for a specific political agenda. Also, his ideas contain their own agenda as he wrote in response to Rousseau's democratic vision and emphasis on popular participation, and he wrote for a French aristocratic audience, not necessarily an American democratic one.

Inherent throughout the discussion of these two themes is yet another essential topic. One that reveals itself in subtle contradictions, and that is often difficult to decipher. As I noted in the previous chapter, it is the dichotomy between our words and actions, between our beliefs and values and how our public lives express these values. The paradox of collective action and the "tragedy of the commons" are common descriptions—in that individual rational behavior has unintended, debilitating collective results—of our contradictory actions. These paradoxes are written into our sacrosanct individual freedoms, and thus our civic virtue debate boils down to the difficulty in reconciling individual liberty with social commitments and obligations. In part, our current troubles focus attention on the difficulty citizens have in understanding their place and roles as individuals and as members of society. For while people learn what their individual rights are in relation to others, and as a buffer against the state, and as players in the market system, people are never instructed about responsibilities to or for others—only in J.S. Mill's negative idea of not impinging upon others' freedoms. Today's civic virtue debate concerns itself with clarifying those commitments and responsibilities, usually by mentioning strong families, schools, church attendance, and community activities. But today's debate, by focusing on the individual, misplaces the onus for creating and sustaining an animated public life. The individual remains at the heart of civic energy, to be sure, but citizens will only realize a vibrant civic life by understanding their actions in the context of all social, political, and economic activity. An individualistic society cannot sustain a viable civic culture.

THE SHAM

My argument is not that civic virtue is an empty debate. Rather, today's debate over civic virtue is empty. Again, today's debate is more a directive. It focuses on societal effects that allow us to throw our collective hands in the air as it creates internal enemies. Also, it does not address the essential problems that produce these social consequences. Take, for example, Gertrude Himmelfarb's recent assessment of the demoralization of American society. Using the Victorian era as an analogous case to compare with America's social conditions, she cites the latter's grim statistics of escalating illegitimacy rates, exponential increases in crime rates, and the dangerous results of welfare dependency as evidence of an unprecedented moral decline. She reports, in a similar period of economic and social change to the one America experiences today, Victorian England "was a more civil, more pacific, more humane society than it had been in the beginning."[1] She summarizes that:

This is the final lesson we may learn from the Victorians: that the ethos of a society, its moral and spiritual character, cannot be reduced to economic, material, political, or other factors, that values—or better yet, virtues—are a determining factor in their own right. So far from being a "reflection," as the Marxist says, of the economic realities, they are themselves, as often as not, the crucial agent in shaping those realities. If in a period of rapid economic and social change, the Victorians managed to achieve a substantial improvement in their "condition" and "disposition," it may be that economic and social change do not necessarily result in personal and public disarray. If they could retain and even strengthen an ethos that had its roots in religion and tradition, it may be that we are not as constrained by the material circumstances of our time as we have thought. A post-industrial economy, we may conclude, does not necessarily entail a postmodernist society or culture.[2]

As evidence of this debate's complexity, Himmelfarb's views are at times insightful and at times limited. Insightful in that she calls attention to the different interpretations that these different times ascribe to individualism. In the Victorian outlook, "the individual . . . was the ally rather than the adversary of society. . . . Self-interest stood not in opposition to the general interest but . . . as the instrument of the general interest. . . . The current notions of self-fulfillment, self-expression, and self-realization derive from a self that does not have to prove itself by reference to any values, purposes, or persons outside itself—that simply is. . . ."[3] In Tocqueville's words, this is the catastrophic difference between individualism rightly and wrongly understood. Catastrophic because individualism wrongly understood is a selfish egoism that saps civic life's resistance to democracy's pitfalls. The question is not what are the consequences of this egoism, such as a lack of moral virtue, rather what are the causes of this wrongly understood individualism?

Himmelfarb's answer to this question is decidedly limited, if not entirely off base. While it may be true that a moral standard guides social action and interaction, and this standard has been challenged by an increasingly individualized society, social policies and a permissive society alone do not account for a complete explanation for this declining morality. In fact, these policies and this permissiveness were once and still remain signs of a societal attempt to redress fundamental inequalities that it determined warranted collective action. Welfare was relief for mothers to care for their children. The so-called permissiveness is the growing recognition of different beliefs and attitudes for celebrating religion, marriage, and other personal choices. When lamenting that these changes have been taken to an extreme, for instance with identity political platforms, and have cost America its civic life, what conservatives like Himmelfarb choose to miss is that these measures were first introduced to counter the effects of other extremes that run rampant in America. Some of these extremes still exist, only in ever increasing disparities: the vast wealth discrepancies between segments of society; the concentration of the economy into high-skilled, high-paying professions and low-paying service jobs; the lack of good educational opportunities for everyone in society; and even modest health care. In fact, today's problems mirror those of America one hundred years ago, revealing that the public policies to remedy those inequities, the policies of which Himmelfarb is so critical, were at best half-hearted attempts or had little lasting impact. The true problem may be political in nature. For the policies conservatives cite as the cause of our civic decline never adequately addressed the social problems they intended to solve. Or, if not only political, economic in nature also, as rough economic equality increasingly becomes more of a utopian vision than a political platform. Or, if not solely political and economic, ideological too, as Americans in principle support free-market policies and disdain governmental action in general. To assume, as Himmelfarb does, that moral standards are at times the sole guiding force for social conditions undervalues all these other interconnected causes, and leaves her analysis decidedly uninformed. In short, Himmelfarb's explanation is limited because she points to ineffective public policies and moral decline as answers to America's wrongly understood individualism, when in fact these ineffective policies and moral decline are symptoms of the pervasive and growing inequalities that foster dismal civic conditions.

To continue, perhaps Victorian England provides a good counter example, but would not America at the turn of the century be a more apt point of reference for today's America? America experienced a Populist political wave followed by the Progressive Era of reform from the late 1880s through the 1910s. However, because the overriding facts of this era were the increased concentration of wealth, the monopolization of industry, the slavish labor practices, the filth of the growing cities, the disdain of immigrants, and the continued oppression of women and minorities, moral turpitude seems a minor factor in the egregious inequities that "advanced" society. In turn, as a society today, what comes first: addressing the illegitimacy rate or the lack of paying jobs, which can support a family? As a society, do we first combat the crime rate with tougher sentences and more prisons, or do we first create more and better educational opportunities for the disadvantaged, unemployed, and displaced workers? As a society, do we first tackle welfare dependency by creating means-testing to reduce roles dramatically, or do we create a business climate that opens opportunities and demands greater community involvement? Like much of today's civic debate, Himmelfarb grasps at the easy answers, to wit her simple critique of Marxists,[4] and she leaves the more socially complex causes and solutions unanswered. Again, the mothers and fathers of illegitimate births, those on welfare, and criminals are Himmelfarb's signs of moral decay—easy targets from which spring solutions that do not involve those who give birth legitimately, those who are able to avoid welfare, and those who do not commit crime. These solutions do not involve most Americans. This is an odd interpretation in that America's moral decay is not caused by the vast majority of Americans, and thus does not demand their attention or action. In some sense, it is a victim mentality, but a victim mentality of the majority.

In addition, as Tocqueville noted, the power of public opinion in the form of the tyranny of the majority robs democracy of its ability to express differences, most especially minority differences. When Himmelfarb criticizes the loss of virtue, she is lamenting the loss of a majority opinion to determine a specific social code. But democracy only thrives when it has a well-spring of difference and dialogue flowing into it. As she should well know, democracy is not just about white, Anglo-Saxon males. To Himmelfarb's credit, though, she does note the disastrous effects of America's ever-increasing individualism, just as Tocqueville forecasted. But to her discredit, she avoids an in-depth analysis of how economic individualism contributes to America's civic decline. By focusing solely on moral action, she misses the American acceptance of materialism and consumerism, the penchant for envying wealth and fame, and the political and social power that money buys. With these socialized beliefs, reiterated by television *ad nauseum*, it seems obvious that Madison Avenue and economic materialism market individualism wrongly understood. Himmelfarb, quite simply then, provides a narrow-sighted cause for our civic decline, one that points to a less government, greater individual initiative agenda without offering any viable reasoning to support such an agenda.

PAST AND PRESENT MYTHS

While Himmelfarb undervalues the economic and political forces that affect America's civic life, she would agree with Michael Sandel's assessment that our political system, as presently structured, cannot foster strong social ties and commitments. At its heart, Sandel's argument is an update of Tocqueville's fears. He argues that America's liberal philosophy predicates itself on a neutral conception of the good life in order to accommodate differences and changing attitudes. Also, rights have replaced any one conception of the good life in order to protect America's distinct social variety. These seemingly benign, or even beneficial, changes have had debilitating civic results. Sandel claims:

Kantian liberals thus avoid affirming a conception of the good by affirming instead the priority of the right, which depends in turn on a picture of the self given prior to its ends. But how plausible is this self-conception? Despite its powerful appeal, the image of the unencumbered self is flawed. It cannot make sense of our moral experience, because it cannot account for certain moral and political obligations that we commonly recognize, even prize. These include obligations of solidarity, religious duties, and other moral ties that may claim us for reasons unrelated to a choice. . . . Conceived as unencumbered selves, we must respect the dignity of all persons, but beyond this, we owe only what we agree to owe. . . . One striking consequence of this view is that "there is no political obligation, strictly speaking, for citizens generally." . . . The average citizen is therefore without any special obligations to his or her fellow citizens, apart from the universal, natural duty not to commit injustice.[5]

Sandel enunciates a common theme in today's political discourse. American liberalism in recent years has prized individual rights to the detriment of communal attachments. Without civic responsibilities, individuals do not attend to their mutual involvement in government and the body politic withers. His communitarian message finds common ground with Himmelfarb's concern about civic and moral decline. They both would agree that American individualism, Sandel's unencumbered self, insulates rather than involves citizens in public dialogue and action.

While Himmelfarb focuses her attention on moral decay, Sandel seeks more governmental initiative and economic change to alter this dismal public path. As he argues, "For despite its appeal, the liberal vision of freedom lacks the civic resources to sustain self-government. This defect ill-equips it to address the sense of disempowerment that afflicts our public life. The public philosophy by which we live cannot secure the liberty it promises, because it cannot inspire the sense of community and civic engagement that liberty requires."[6]

Conservatives and communitarians alike agree that individualism is a key element to America's civic decline. But are there more factors than America's increasing individualism to explain its lack of civic vitality? Certainly, the conservative perspective falls silent about individual behavior in market and political actions, and thus their condemnation of individualism seems stunted or duplicitous. Also, while communitarians recognize the need for business reform and a role for government in inculcating public virtue, it remains an open question whether Americans would support changes that limit some of their cherished freedoms. Has America reached a socio-political impasse where the freedoms they have come to expect conflict with the social ties and obligations necessary for a workable democracy? Or even more to the point, do the freedoms Americans expect from their social and political systems undermine the ability of these systems to ensure these freedoms? Sandel believes this is the case, and insight into this unique social condition can offer insight into how to solve this dilemma.

A starting point to examine America's unique and difficult civic quandary begins with the foundations of and changes in American ideology, both socially and politically. Himmelfarb notes how virtues, either in the Victorian sense or in the classical or Christian view, devolved into more uncertain, individualized values in the modern, late nineteenth century era. Sandel describes how the legal system has incorporated this system of rights without obligations throughout the twentieth century. Alisdair MacIntyre notes how values and opinions preclude any concept of right and wrong, good and bad so that public dialogue can never find common ground. Americans are left talking "past each other"; or in other words, civic topics and debate remain incommensurable.[7] If, then, one of the first problems is the inability to find even meager common assumptions, then public debate appears impossible. Consequently, most contentious public issues, and many private ones too, ultimately have their hearing only in court. As Jean Bethke Elshtain describes it, this 'juridical model of democracy' "is black and white, winner-take-all. This [model], first pushed by liberal activists and now embraced by their conservative counterparts . . . preempts democratic contestation and a politics of respect and melioration."[8] Daniel Kemmis notes that one of the remaining moments of democratic politics, the public hearing, is neither public, as private interests preclude common understanding, nor a hearing, as sides continue to press their claims and refuse to listen.[9] With this relativized, rights-oriented backdrop, the question is How has this liberal philosophy and growing individualism affected civic virtue?

To answer this question, though, I need to give civic virtue a more precise definition. The phrase harkens back to democracy's infancy, perhaps in classical times, when rights were not citizens' foremost preoccupation. If, as Aristotle thought, man was by nature political, and the object of the polis was the good life, then a certain character was necessary to secure this good. Virtues were the recognition and the practice of choosing to live within extremes. Wisdom, temperance, justice, and courage were the most heralded virtues of the Classical Era,[10] while Christian scholars later added to or supplanted these, depending on the philosopher, with faith, hope, and charity. To gloss over years of debate, the overriding theme is that philosophers for centuries saw a close connection between individual action and society's health. Civic virtue was the public action of engaged citizens, motivated to help each other as the expression of their knowledge that healthy, involved individuals make for a healthy society and a government of moderate means and ends. It is simply the concern for more than oneself and one's immediate interests—knowing that one's interests exist within a larger framework of collective concerns and goals. Today, this concern for collective interests is what many feel America lacks. Robert Putnam avoids the contentiousness of the word virtue when he argues America's "social capital" has diminished dramatically. But the inference is clear that our civic attitudes and actions are lacking and this has led to an empty public life. An empty public life undermines democracy as the people lose their power of self-rule to perhaps an omnipresent, intrusive state or ruler.

The battleground of today's debate is between individual rights and any conception of the good life. It is between issue-oriented or identity political platforms and any concern for public interests. It is between narrow interests that override any moral or ethical ideology. As is obvious, it is clear that granting the former interests in the name of rights displaces the latter's concern for democracy in general. As is also obvious, it is much easier to satisfy the aims of individual rights, individual platforms, and narrowly defined interests in comparison to what is meant by the vague phrases of public good and collective morality. Washington representatives reveal this political fact as each scrambles to satisfy their individual constituencies as the national or public interest falls by the wayside. As pork-barreling precedes controlling the national debt, private interests take political precedence over collective issues. Also, history shows that public goods and morals often involve a degree of oppression and intolerance, such as policies against immigrants, homosexuals, the propertyless, and even women in general. Rogers M. Smith carefully describes how periods in American history witness the institutionalization of specific civic agendas, often to the detriment of large numbers in society.[11] These public agendas have been decried as a tyranny of the majority, and in a democracy increasingly careful to protect individual rights, they have over time been called into question as the enemy of diversity, openness, and respect for difference.

Individualism, or Tocqueville's wrongly understood conception of individualism, is the social element that most often spurs cries of civic decline. But in a political system that caters to individualized careers and programs, despite the Republican revolution in 1994, and in an economic system that champions individual tastes, although ironically to a mass audience, and in a society predicated on individual initiative and freedom, it seems foolish to assume Americans would act any other way but with an individualism wrongly understood. Tocqueville, though, was far more optimistic about America's possibilities. While he was concerned about individualism's unchecked power in a society becoming more and more equal, he wrote, "I do not think . . . that there is more egoism among us [the French] than in America; the only difference is that there it is enlightened. . . . Every American has the sense to sacrifice some of his private interests to save the rest." But Tocqueville follows such optimism with careful reservations, explaining, "If citizens, attaining equality, were to remain ignorant and coarse, it would be difficult to foresee any limit to the stupid excesses into which their selfishness might lead them. . . . I do not think that the doctrine of self-interest as preached in America is in all respects self-evident. . . ."[12] His cautious appraisal, though, allows for great leeway in contemporary theorizing as all sorts of commentators invoke his views today.

If Tocqueville is the accepted historical reference point for today's social crisis, then are his observations about American society accurate? This question pertains not just to today's cultural application, which seems difficult to fathom given the intervening century and a half, but also for his observations of America in the 1830s. For if he misread America's tendencies then, today's applicability is cast in great doubt. For instance, Barry Alan Shain determines that:

> Political individualism is not a goal toward which Americans intentionally strove in [the past two centuries], but instead is the unintended end product of multiple failures. Such creative historical accounting is troubling not only because it has falsely reified individualism into America's chosen political ideology, but because, as a consequence, a long and rich tradition of American political thought has been ignored. What has been largely overlooked is a normative theory of the good political life that is enduring, democratic, and communal. . . . America's Protestant, democratic, and communal localism, however, is its most enduring political tradition.[13]

Individualism as the unwanted result of repeated failure to achieve other ends? Calling Tocqueville's views misguided, Shain argues that America's history is one of failed attempts at self-sacrifice to Christian beliefs, or for moral rectitude, or to one's family, work, and community. In his mind, it is only in the latter half of the twentieth century that individualism has become the dominant political ideology. When Tocqueville observed American society, his notion of an American individualism was only in comparison to his tradition-bound, aristocratic, entrenched French homeland. If Tocqueville read American society only in reference to his French background, it is not assured that his views can apply accurately to America either then or today.

In addition, Shain raises the larger, disturbing issue of civic myths. With his claim that American individualism is a myth that re-crafts historical fact, Shain argues that Americans do not know who they are. Or, because they do not hold to a past, America has the ability to recast itself as it sees fit. Thus, America remains culturally adrift and prone to dubious visions of its grandeur and of its failings, and America, given its ignorance, is prone to the nefarious whims of leaders. Shain states, "More disconcerting, however, than my realization that we are a people enjoying a limited republican inheritance and a more questionable liberal foundation has been my recognition that we are a people without a past. As a people, we have consistently re-created our past."[14] If Shain is correct, then America's penchant for re-creation makes today's use of Tocqueville highly problematic.

Rogers M. Smith adds theoretical weight to Shain's contention. He notes one role of society's leaders is to create civic myths. As the phrase implies, these myths have an element of truth interwoven with complete fabrication. Over time, it may be difficult to know which element is which, and which adds to the myth's power and legitimacy. Smith writes:

> As Plato suggested long ago, the stories of civic identity fostered by political elites are virtually always false or at least highly dubious in important respects. . . . Because no community or leadership is simply natural, . . . leaders usually foster loyalty by playing as many psychological chords as possible. They worry less about whether their various appeals are true, or whether they fit together logically, than about whether they work politically. They thus simultaneously appeal to lofty rational moralities and thinly veiled greed and lust for power. But most have found irreplaceable the engaging, reassuring, inspiring, often intoxicating charm provided by colorful civic myths.[15]

My point is to call into question America's so-called accepted belief in its individualistic nature. If America is truly not the culture that today's civic critics tell us it is, then perhaps their agenda reveals itself. Also, to ask what America was and what America is today also allows for a basic examination of Tocqueville's ideas and whether his ideas can be useful for a productive civic discussion. Thus, a little history may allow me to uncover some repeated errors in American thinking. While civic virtue is the enlightened cry for building a strong democracy, the myths that swirl around this concept seem to add confusion rather than insight into its nature and possibilities.

TOCQUEVILLE DISSECTED

Given Tocqueville's prominence in today's civic debate, a wealth of research has amassed that calls for a clearer understanding of his ideas.

The research falls into two categories. One questions both his historical accuracy and subsequent interpretation of American society. Another employs an ideological and cultural review and clarifies Tocqueville's mythic and misguided stature as America's emblematic democratic proponent. Both approaches state that Tocqueville, despite his many insights about American society, provides a narrow view of what America truly was at the time. Thus, since he has become the intellectual democratic icon for both the Right and the Left over the several generations, then his limited observations are ripe for societal misinterpretation and political machination. In a sense, then, it may be apt that social conservatives employ Tocqueville as their democratic visionary, as they too provide a vision of America that has applied only to a select segment of society and allows for few choices for most Americans.

Skocpol's critique of Tocqueville concentrates on Tocqueville's observation that the national government appeared non-existent in the workings of daily life. He argued that Americans conducted their democratic affairs at an immediate, local level. The numerous civic associations that took the place of any centralized administration promised that people would remain wedded to the common good and involved in civic and political interests. The result was an active democratic culture and a minimalist state. From the eyes of a French observer, where centralization and bureaucracy were the norms, this lack of national power was not only astonishing but ennobling. Skocpol, though, notes that Tocqueville misses the effects of the U.S. Postal Service in nurturing the development of associational life in communities throughout America. Its effects include not just the simple tying together of communities. Rather, the postal service served political interests in several capacities. Skocpol states:

Obviously the institutional structure of the U.S. government had everything to do with the spread of the postal network. The legislative system gave senators and—above all—members of the House of Representatives a strong interest in subsidizing communication and transportation links into even the remotest areas of the growing nation. U.S. postal rules allowed for the free exchange of newspapers among editors, allowing small newspapers to pick up copy from bigger ones. . . . Congress could use its frank and the postal system to communicate freely with citizens. In turn, citizens . . . could readily communicate with one another, monitoring the doings of Congress and state legislatures as well as those of local government. Voluntary associations soon learned to put out their message in "newspaper" formats to take advantage of the mail. . . . Emergent political parties in Jacksonian America were intertwined with the federal postal system. Party entrepreneurs were often newspaper editors and postmasters. . . . [Finally] one of the first great moral reform movements in America . . . was devoted to stop the opening of post offices and transportation of the mails on Sundays.[16]

Most importantly for today's civic debate, Skocpol believes it is most accurate to conclude that associations and America's nascent democratic culture were fostered by the interaction of civic groups, federal action, and many other societal changes and cultural factors. While Tocqueville acknowledges many of these factors, like the influence religion and free newspapers had on building communal ties, other factors that he mentions, like America's significant degree of political participation, are often discounted by the leading exponents of his thought. Conservatives applaud Tocqueville's idea that a minimalist state is to democracy's benefit, but many never acknowledge that his applause for thorough political participation demands dramatic changes today, and most likely under federal government regulation. Again, today many see only what they want to see in Tocqueville's ideas. Interestingly, then, while Skocpol notes that both Republicans and Democrats today "have converged on a vision of minimal national governance and vibrant local voluntary associations,"[17] they are as limited in their views just as Tocqueville "was blinded by his experiences with, and negative passions about, state power in France."[18]

Skocpol raises another point that is open to scrutiny. She argues, in contrast to Tocqueville's view that associational life focused on local interests and politics, that the evidence suggests associational groups of all types, both local and translocal, have developed throughout America's history. She writes, "Not only were most of the encompassing voluntary associations in U.S. history founded before 1900, but over a fifth of those we have identified so far were launched before the Civil War. . . . Even if we leave aside political parties and churches, very large numbers of Americans were clearly working together through translocal associations from very early in our history. . . . [Also] foundings of big associations are remarkably spread out over the entire life of the nation."[19] If correct, it seems that large associations necessitate a broader, more national public outlook. Tocqueville, however, emphasized only America's inward-looking, local discourse.

Shain adds more fuel to this discrepancy as he argues that Tocqueville confused localism with his newly-coined term of individualism. The two should not be confused, for localism was the historical legacy and the political genius of American associational life. But for Tocqueville, unfamiliar with this form of social and political interaction given his French background, localism was both a beneficial and potentially destructive element for democracy. For, as Shain argues, Tocqueville thought individualism, with its damaging possibilities, was localism in another form. He claims, "Is a public and virtuous life for Tocqueville not equivalent to national life? If so, there would be little separation between local communal and private egoistic life in his mind. By having conflated local communalism with true individualism, he was moved to attribute to American communalism those very ills against which it had successfully fought, in some cases, for two centuries."[20] Several inferences emerge from Shain's thesis. The most immediate is that, just as Skocpol notes, Tocqueville's background directed his thinking to highlight aspects of American democracy that were exaggerations of current reality. American society was less individualistic than Tocqueville described given its strong communal, religious, and moral attachments. However, American society was much more individualistic than Tocqueville's French homeland. The point, then, that both Skocpol and Shain emphasize is that Tocqueville's views cannot be taken as wholly accurate because his background colors his interpretations.

Shain argues that familism, particularism, and communalism were the dominant characteristics of eighteenth century America. Tocqueville, among others, misleadingly labeled society individualistic because the diversity between stringent moral communities allowed for an inadvertent degree of individual freedom.[21] What Tocqueville witnessed, then, was not individualism because of the degree of local control over individual behavior. Each community established powerfully strong codes of behavior to limit individual expression. Individual differences emerged between the strictness of the communities, not as an expression of individual preferences. Tocqueville, then, witnessed some measure of difference only because of the numerous communities that existed, and especially in relation to the staid, aristocratic uniformity to which he was accustomed. Shain's point is that communities produced a type of individualism, but not the type of individualism where citizens are capable of expressing their views apart from their social situation and protected by rights. At base, Shain infers that Tocqueville mistakenly characterizes American society as individualistic.

Moreover, while Shain notes America's strong localism at this time, Skocpol's research recognizes that numerous translocal groups existed. This apparent discrepancy is resolved, though, if Shain's notion of diversity between communities, rather than differences between individuals, is understood. Skocpol seeks to argue that American society was not as thoroughly localized or inward-looking as Tocqueville and common ideology assumes it to have been. These connections between distant communities and their distant political or civic representatives makes her case. Shain's point, though, is that the dominant characteristic of American life in the early eighteenth century was locally-centered. It can be true that both are accurate—most of the activity of the community involved local issues— although some of those issues transferred to a larger constituency outside of the locale's immediate scope. If nothing else these differing interpretations show that Tocqueville's ideas of a strong individualism cannot be employed unequivocally. To assume that American society was wholly individualistic at the time when Tocqueville described it as such is a gross reporting error. To employ this conception for political ends today does a historical disservice to the period in question while it satisfies an overly simplistic characterization toward disingenuous ends.

Shain's ideas also offer an ideological discrepancy between America's civic understanding and its history. America's individualistic heritage reveals more about a foreigner's colored observations than about American society. He claims, "The vast majority of Americans lived voluntarily in morally demanding agricultural communities shaped by reformed-Protestant social and moral norms. These communities were defined by overlapping circles of family- and community-assisted self-regulation and even self-denial, rather than by individual autonomy and self-defining political activity."[22] Less than a half century later, Tocqueville traveled America and witnessed similar patterns of social and cultural interaction. The national government remained at a distance, and the economy was primarily agricultural. Strong religious directives, a strict moral code, and established communal ties created a civic life based on individual responsibility to the community's interests. Individualism existed, to be sure, but Tocqueville's emphasis on individualism must be viewed from the French experience of a centralized, administrative state. Shain's research gives credence to the idea that America's understanding of itself may be illusionary and based on well-rehearsed civic myths.

As evidence of this mythical past, Smith notes that Tocqueville's thesis is simply too narrow in its discussion of American political and social history. What is missing from Tocqueville's vantage point? In general, the treatment of women and non-European peoples are not recognized. The propertyless and their lack of social, economic, and political power find no hearing. Smith notes that Tocqueville's argument centers on one principal characteristic of American society, that of a "growing equality of conditions." However, Smith claims this equality of conditions is an erroneous description with far-reaching historical and ideological consequences. He states:

The Tocquevillian story . . . is centered on relationships among a minority of Americans (white men, largely of northern European ancestry) analyzed via reference to categories derived from the hierarchy of political and economic statuses men have held in Europe. . . . But the comparative moral, material, and political egalitarianism that prevailed at the founding among propertied white men was surrounded by an array of other fixed, ascriptive systems of unequal status. . . . Men were thought naturally suited to rule over women, within both the family and the polity. White northern Europeans were thought superior culturally—and probably biologically—to black Africans, bronze Native Americans, and indeed all other races and civilizations. Many British Americans also treated religion as an inherited condition and regarded Protestants as created by God to be morally and politically, as well as theologically, superior to Catholics, Jews, Muslims, and others. . . . These beliefs were not merely emotional prejudices or "attitudes." *Over time, American intellectual and political elites elaborated distinctive justifications for these ascriptive systems, including inegalitarian scriptural readings, the scientific racism of the "American school" of ethnology, racial and sexual Darwinism, and the romantic cult of Anglo-Saxonism in American historiography.*[23]

Smith delivers several important themes. One is that Tocqueville's historical interpretation of American civic life is limited. Thus, to employ his observations to contemporary society upholds patterns of unjust moral and political behavior. In fact, to employ his observations to contemporary society misses some of the most enlightened democratic steps America has ever taken in its history, by expanding the popular vote and providing broad legal protection for more citizens. Another theme that Smith offers is that our ideological underpinnings are tenuous at best. To be certain, America has a history of civic participation that is unique to its democratic experience. At the same time, it also has a history of racism, sexism, and dogmatic conformity that existed as an important component of its civic life. Smith only seeks to have both elements receive proper and proportionate explanation. To emphasize one without the other misses historical fact and the important changes American society has adopted since Tocqueville's writings. In this sense, perhaps the prestige and power of American civic life may be in its changes since Tocqueville, rather than in what Tocqueville mistakenly observed. Finally, this idea allows for the conjecture that America's civic understanding is itself constrained. It is hampered by America's own civic myths. If we rely on Tocqueville's misreading or on some present-day political agenda to call attention to America's civic past, surely these observations and today's civic virtue debate hide an inegalitarian past. It allows historical fact to go unheeded, and in this case applauded for its significant changes, while it allows civic myths to perpetuate false characterizations of individualism and of civic decline. Ironically, then, by invoking Tocqueville Americans remain ignorant of their own creative civic developments, and they only hear the cries of decline from political operatives.

Tocqueville wrote that what propels American democracy is its growing equality of conditions; however, for many Americans, political equality would not exist for scores of decades, and economic equality was an
out-and-out chimera for most. In an exhaustive study of the economic
wealth of eighteenth and early nineteenth century America, Lee Soltow
favors the interpretation that American society was far less equal than as
it is today. This striking observation, given pronounced significance with
the marked concentration of American wealth since the Reagan presidency,
further discounts Tocqueville's ideas about a growing equality of conditions. Soltow writes:

The hypothesis that there was relative equality of wealth in the early United
States is the central and pervasive issue that I have investigated . . . in an attempt to
subject the perceptions of Tocqueville and others to quantitative proof. . . . Prominent in [Tocqueville's] analysis was the belief that inequality *was decreasing*, in the
main, from generation to generation. . . . One can contest the Tocqueville thesis
...The distribution of real estate in 1798 has intriguing attributes. First and foremost is the fact that 433,000—or almost exactly half, of America's 877,000 free males
21 years and older—owned real estate. . . . The top ten percent of adult male wealth
holders held almost half of all wealth. The top 5 percent controlled almost a third of
wealth. This is substantial inequality. . . . Inequality of wealth in America was accepted largely because it was so much less than in Europe. . . . In the data there is a
strong implication that the economic well-being of Americans is much more homo-
geneous today than it was two centuries ago.[24]

Again, Tocqueville's ideas are meaningful only if they are viewed in relation to aristocratic Europe. America had what Benjamin Franklin described
as a "happy mediocrity" and a greater potential for material comfort than
Europe at the time, but even a rough equality was nonexistent for most
people. Soltow's work shows that in an age before industrialization, ur-
banization, and the movement from an agricultural to an industrial base,
American society was still vastly unequal. To assume otherwise—some
commentators herald America's agricultural period as a land of equality
and political participation—simply overlooks the stark social reality.
America, since its inception, has always been home to vast inequalities in
all social, economic, and political arenas. To believe Tocqueville's observations plays into perceptions that feed civic myths.

In addition, Tocqueville argued that social equality was a new power in
the modern, democratic world, one that demanded great vigilance as it
could easily undermine essential liberty. As he described how a majority
tyrannizes with the subversive power of popular opinion, he sought to
maintain the freedoms of difference and diversity that derive from typi-

cally the "better" classes. By arguing against majority tyranny and preserving the rights of a minority, in his time Tocqueville thought it important to maintain the freedoms of the privileged, aristocratic class. Repeatedly, Tocqueville sees democracy's and equality's leveling effects, and while he praises them, he also warns that too much of them destroys the uniqueness of difference, exalted refinement, cherished virtue, and acts of great achievement. Today, however, safeguarding against majority tyranny is employed by groups who have been left out of the policy process, or who often have no social, economic, or political clout. Over time, then, the view of majority tyranny has changed from the emotional mob rule of popular democracy willing to run roughshod over tradition and liberty—that was America's founding fathers' and Tocqueville's fear. The popular conception today is that majority tyranny applies to the oppressive culture of middle-class morality willing to limit basic freedoms of minority views. So, while both periods speak about preserving liberty against majority tyranny, Tocqueville's minority is that of the rich and privileged while today's minority is that of the oppressed and disadvantaged. If for no other reason, this change in whose liberty must be protected again shows the inapplicability of Tocqueville's ideas for today's civic virtue debate. It is not the privileged and wealthy who must be protected economically and politically. They are the ones who participate the most, who have the most influence in today's systems of influence. It also shows, again, the significant strides America has made in rectifying those social and legal injustices that Smith notes.

TOCQUEVILLE'S RELEVANCE

Just as I argue that today's conservative-led civic virtue debate needs greater subtlety in understanding how civic life emerges and what solutions are possible, my focus on Tocqueville's historical accuracy needs greater subtlety too. For, some argue, Tocqueville's benefit does not come from a thoroughly accurate portrayal of American society. The civic debate may not need a precise historical accounting, rather it must be more concerned with a realistic account of what American society has become. From this perspective, Tocqueville's description of individualism and its detrimental effects on society's functioning, his recognition of the importance of civic groups in curbing individualistic tendencies, and his ideas that strong civic groups buffer essential individual liberties from an intrusive state, resonate strongly in popular thinking about America's post-industrial, materialistic, and bureaucratic staples. With active civic groups, Tocqueville also provides an answer to today's often maddening economic and political times. His ideas, then, are important to consider and apply to contemporary politics. The issue worth criticizing, as I hope I have developed, is how present-day politicians and social commentators employ Tocqueville's worthy insights.

While his ideas are worthy of study and analysis, they are also limited in significant ways. First, as many on both the Right and the Left criticize society for its individualistic behavior, very little action is taken to curb this behavior. Because individualism centers on the individual, the stone that is cast becomes one of a moral dictate and thus more reserved for religious or social control. It is not that conservatives and liberals disagree unequivocally over developing strong families, creating viable school systems, curbing crime and drugs, and fostering energetic communities. It is just that conservatives employ a creed that selectively disparages behavior in one realm, such as the freedom to abortion, when they exalt similar freedoms in another realm, such as the unrestrained ability to make money. More importantly, individualism underscores American economic behavior. More frequently today political success depends upon individualized careers catering to specific constituents for reelection, rather than attachment to a platform espoused by a political party. Mavericks rule the day while society bears the collective cost of their individualism.

A second shortcoming of Tocqueville's views center on the current political siren for reducing the size of the federal government. Most politicians and researchers agree that its largesse fuels inefficiency, and its distance discourages citizen input and action. Tocqueville's idea that civic groups are the source of democratic success seems prudent, practical, historically legitimate, and politically agreeable. Even most liberals today would agree that welfare is a mess because of the federal government's handling. But Skocpol's research reveals that Tocqueville misread the presence and influential guidance of the federal government in America's history. She also notes that America was less locally centered as its civic myths articulate. Many civic groups had regional and national ties, spurred on by the federal postal system and the increasing ease of communication and flow of information. From Skocpol, the view to downsize the federal government may be just an easy target, one that finds and misguides popular opinion in the name of an under-researched political agenda.

Third, and why Tocqueville's ideas need distance from today's civic debate agenda, the notion of strong civic participation as the fundamental element of a democratic society is the cornerstone of Tocqueville's thought. However, often this idea of all citizens interacting politically is not part of today's civic debate. Tocqueville wrote, "It is by taking a share in legislation that the American learns to know the law; it is by governing that he becomes educated about the formalities of government.[25] . . . It is clear that unless each citizen learned to combine with his fellows to preserve his freedom at a time when he individually is becoming weaker and so less able in isolation to defend it, tyranny would be bound to increase with equality."[26] While current civic debate focuses on the implication of group action and interaction, my emphasis is on Tocqueville's choice of the word *each*. This sense of inclusion and extensive political action finds no parallel from the conservative perspective. Instead, they concentrate on reestablishing communal moral standards, such as anti-homosexual messages, which exclude some citizens' views from the political process.

Fourth, and finally, Tocqueville argues that civic action is the political expression of a deeper, more influential commitment within communities. He speaks of well-established habits, customs, traditions, and mores as the definitive elements that ensure vibrant civic action. He writes, "I have said . . . that I considered mores to be one of the great general causes responsible for the maintenance of a democratic republic in the United States. . . . I mean [mores] to apply not only to '*moeurs*' in the strict sense, which might be called the habits of the heart, but also to the different notions possessed by men, the various opinions current among them, and the sum of ideas that shaped mental habits."[27] This concern for morals and habits sits well with the popular agenda of decrying America's lack of morality and making lists of what morals have been lost and thus are now necessary. William Bennett's *The Book of Virtues* is one of the most popular examples, and Himmelfarb's and Charles Murray's work repeats similar themes. As Robert Bork informs us, "Is censorship really as unthinkable as we all seem to assume? That it is unthinkable is a very recent conceit. From the earliest colonies on this continent over 300 years ago, and for about 175 years of our existence as a nation, we endorsed and lived with censorship."[28] Bork's statement should help us realize that any return to a past societal norm is not just impossible but foolish. The trenchant point, however, is that if some citizens are excluded from the political process, if economic equality excludes others still, and if social equality belies long-standing prejudices, which are in fact habits and customs too, then mores are a double-edged sword. They can be used to foster inequality and anti-democratic views as well as democratic ones. As Smith claims, "Liberal democratic norms have often been unreflective if not irrational sets of beliefs, just as deserving of the label 'prejudices' as racial values."[29] Habits and customs are essential, but today's civic debate is not inclusive enough to elicit support from all segments of society. In turn, it seems a majority tyrannizes by stifling collective thought and action.

Despite these objections, Tocqueville has much of worth to say about America's current civic discussion. The task is to separate what Tocqueville meant from what commentators employ his words to mean. For to better understand his words discourages one of his greatest fears, that of the tyranny of majority opinion. He writes that, "We need seek no other reason for the absence of great writers in America so far; literary genius cannot exist without freedom of the spirit, and there is no freedom of the spirit in America." Tocqueville sees the compromises inherent in democratic republics. He claims that while democracy and equality grant small, simple pleasures to each man every day, they do so by forsaking great undertakings and sublime achievements. Why does Tocqueville sense a lack of spirit in democratic times? He believes that majority opinion has the unrestrained power to control behavior. As men seek acceptance and inclusion and do not pursue exalted endeavors, democracy and equality tend to moderate social behavior. Because many have some wealth and influence in their circles, none is thought of as better. Each then is moderate in attitudes and actions, and each seeks to fit in with the current democratic times. Tocqueville continues, "One finds governments striving to protect mores by condemning the authors of licentious books. No one in the United States is condemned for works of that sort, but no one is tempted to write them. . . . In this, no doubt, power is well used, but my point is that nature of the power itself. This *irresistible power* is a continuous fact and *its good use only an accident.*"[30] Tocqueville argues that majority opinion has no social or political check. Much like the Madisonian realization that good statesmen will not always lead America, Tocqueville believes that majority opinion can fashion unjust as well as just policies. But while the founding fathers built institutional checks to monitor poor leadership, majority opinion has little constraint in controlling social action. Moreover, he calls into question the oft-repeated refrain of the majority's judiciousness. As Smith noted above, majorities are equally capable of instituting prejudices and racism. But majority opinion has unbridled power in its numbers, and so while it has the disturbing ability to create unjust policies, it has the even more powerful role of silencing dissension and maintaining conformity to these unjust policies. Majority tyranny, for Tocqueville, is thus a more subtle, more pervasive, and more debilitating tyranny than any other.

A form of majority tyranny insinuates itself into the current civic virtue debate. By casting America's principal failings as failings of morals and virtues, this approach takes a "high road" that provides few sources of social and political response. Why implicate "corrupt" individuals as the source of social decline? Because the problem remains abstract or distant enough, or individualized enough not to necessitate political action, and the conservative agenda has built a powerful platform on limiting political, especially federal, action. If the problem is crime, build more jails. If the issue is welfare, means-test to reduce the roles. If the concern is drugs, then make stricter laws and enforce them thoroughly. These solutions never address the systems, the institutions, nor the processes that foster these problems, and they leave the future of American society in grave uncertainty too.

As an example, take the robust demand for devolving power away from the federal government. Chided for its inefficiency and bureaucracy, big government remains an easy target to cast as undermining democracy. But direct democracy has its chinks too, as California's initiative process reveals a more open but out of control process. Garry Wills reports, "The state's punitive measures against immigrants and their children have been checked by the courts, have backfired against their sponsors and have unsettled candidates dependent on Hispanic or Asian voters. Draconian term limits (six years for Assembly members) were supposed to curtail careerism, the power of special interests, cronyism and the lobbyists' sway—but have increased all four."[31] Wisconsin's form of centralized planning, led by Governor Tommy Thompson, may be a better example of a state's ability to coordinate and implement power. But Wills cites disturbing anti-democratic instincts within Thompson's agenda. He claims, "Thompson is certainly not a champion of localism if that means cities or counties or the State Legislature can defy his general strategy. He boasts of the 290 items he vetoed in the first budget submitted by the Legislature. . . . Thompson sometimes makes fun of Washington 'know-it-alls' who could not pass his 'Elroy test' (what his little hometown knows is good for it). But Thompson also boasts of his reliance on experts, called in from all quarters to help him with planning. One of those experts, Lawrence Mead, wants to make welfare 'the new paternalism,' frankly telling people what is good for them. Temperamentally, Thompson is inclined to such hectoring certitude. . . ."[32] My point is not that state power and initiative is an aberrant choice, only that criticism of the federal government carries public opinion too easily. Only with the democratic difficulties in California and only with Thompson's underlying moral dictates is it obvious that the federal government's power may be a product, and a necessary product too, of more dastardly processes.

What may be those other dastardly processes? Paul Hawken explains the complexity behind the federal government's size when he analyzes the relationship between big government and big business. The interesting fact is that while big government is the butt of jokes and the object of public criticism, big business receives relatively little negative press, perhaps because of its revered position in American ideology. Hawken, though, sees an interconnected mix between the two that produces stalemate. He describes the process as:

> Business assumes the role of guardianship vis-à-vis the ecosystem and fails miserably in the task; governance steps in to try to mitigate the damage; business tries to sabotage this regulatory process and nimbly sidesteps those regulations that *are* put on the books; governance ups the ante and thereby becomes a hydra-headed bureaucratic monster choking off economic development while squandering money; business decries "interference in the marketplace" and sets out to redress its grievances by further corrupting the legislative and regulatory process in an attempt to become *de facto* guardian, if not *de jure*.[33]

David C. Korten concludes from Hawken's analysis that "the bigger our corporations, the greater their power to externalize costs and the greater the need for big government to protect the public interest and to clean up the consequent social and environmental messes. The more we cut our giant corporations down to human scale, the more we will be able to reduce the size of big business."[34] Corporate power is so unequivocal and pervasive that any social and political platform that seeks to downsize corporations seems ludicrous and anti-American. Yet, the platform to downsize the government has achieved such backing it has become one of those tired campaign cliches: "If elected, I shall cut government size and inefficiency."

Again, we assess and predict our social, economic, and political future with quick, easy answers. Thompson's invocation of morality displaces the messiness of politics with solutions that gloss over what new troubles will replace the old. Action for the sake of acting does not offer optimal outcomes. Tocqueville recognized that America displayed a penchant for activity, the bustle that comes from civic and business interaction, but he understood too that this bustle was constrained by the people's preoccupation with equality and wealth. In a sense in democratic times policies change constantly to tinker with the system, but the changes are always relatively the same. And Tocqueville notes who has an advantage in these times and in these policies. He writes, "When every citizen is independent of and indifferent to the rest, the cooperation of each of them can only be obtained by paying for it; this infinitely multiplies the purpose to which wealth may be applied and increases its value."[35] Corporate wealth, then, buys the system. In turn, it provides a marketed view for Americans to feel a bit relieved in that their views fall in step with majority opinion, and thus this agreement fuels either complacency or unexamined social servitude. What takes the place of informed, democratic debate if marketed majority opinion fosters these conditions? Most often, civic myths maintain majority control and citizen acquiescence.

Is, then, as I hint at in this chapter, America's civic virtue one of its civic myths? The answer can be an honest no, as American society has a history of strong communal ties. Greider's few examples that I noted earlier can be multiplied in community after community across the country. My father's example is repeated countless times when issues strike citizens close to home or when they act upon a discernible need. Moreover, my father's initiative shows that self-interest cannot explain all civic behavior. Many times, people act out of the goodness of their hearts for the benefit of all. However, the answer can also be a strong yes, as American individualism as the basis of American independence, initiative, and prosperity may very well be a myth. But the myth may be that our civic tradition is overly dramatized simply because it was necessary to survive by joining with others on the frontier farm or in the burgeoning big city. Again, perhaps we need to understand our civic virtue as we have come to understand Tocqueville. Only in relation to other countries, times, and democracies, do we see the value of our civic interaction. But if our civic life was perhaps necessary for social and political survival, especially after a war of independence and then again with England in 1812, can we accurately label a necessity virtuous? It seems only if the behavior has beneficial results, and thus only with hindsight, can we assess its benefits. Perhaps, today our hindsight invokes a time with mythic virtue when in fact the behavior was not virtuous at all, merely socially and politically expedient.

Finally, though, let me provide a third choice for the civic virtue as civic myth question. This choice sees the power of virtuous behavior as defined by a community reinforcing like-minded behavior. These behaviors establish attitudes and create traditions of public service and collective identity. In turn, this sense of community generates an ideology, sometimes referred to less rigorously as a myth, that finds similar expression at distant parts of the same country. The ideology or myth gives explanatory power to behavior that is unique in its effects. Or, the myth gives undue weight to behavior that exemplifies a spirit or initiative that fuels beneficial results, and yet realistically contributes only at times and under specific circumstances. It gives explanatory power to traditions, customs, habits, and Tocqueville's *moeurs* that create and sustain social conditions. Perhaps, myths are rubber bands of reality, stretching historical accuracy to satisfy other important social conditions, those of social psychic or collective attitudinal qualities. Without these myths, societies may simply lose sight of their self-defined importance and function, and lose their desire to continue on together. One of America's myths, as Tocqueville wrote, has been its relative equality of economic conditions. It is to this equality and its mythic power to which I now turn to give more insight to today's civic conditions.

NOTES

1. Gertrude Himmelfarb, *The De-Moralization of Society: From Victorian Virtues to Modern Values* (New York: Alfred A. Knopf, 1995), 255.

2. Ibid., 257.

3. Ibid., 256.

4. Ibid., 254. Himmelfarb states Marx's idea that the industrial-bourgeois revolution would reduce all relations to "cash transactions" was wrong because of the strong influence Victorian virtues had in everyday English Victorian life. However, Tocqueville provides an equally compelling alternative to Himmelfarb's criticism. He states, "Men living in democratic times have many passions, but most of these cultivate in love of wealth or derive from it. That is not because their souls are narrower but because money really is more important at such times. . . . Distinction based on wealth is increased by the disappearance of diminution of all other distinctions." Tocqueville, *Democracy in America*, 614–615.

5. Michael J. Sandel, *Democracy's Discontent: America in Search of a Public Philosophy* (Cambridge, Mass.: The Belknap Press of Harvard University Press, 1996), 13–14.

6. Ibid., 6.

7. Alisdair MacIntyre, *After Virtue* (Notre Dame, Ind.: University of Notre Dame Press, 1984), 8.

8. Jean Bethke Elshtain, *Democracy on Trial* (New York: Basic Books, 1995), 27.

9. Daniel Kemmis, *Community and the Politics of Place* (Norman, Okla.: University of Oklahoma Press, 1990), 53.

10. Aristotle, *The Politics*, translated by T. A. Sinclair (Baltimore, Md.: Penguin Books, 1962), 114, 144.

11. Rogers M. Smith, *Civic Ideals: Conflicting Visions of Citizenship in U. S. History* (New Haven: Yale University Press, 1997), 5–12.

12. Alexis de Tocqueville, *Democracy in America*, 527–528.

13. Barry Alan Shain, *The Myth of American Individualism: The Protestant Origins of American Political Thought* (Princeton, N.J.: Princeton University Press, 1994), xviii.

14. Ibid., xvii.

15. Rogers M. Smith, *Civic Ideals*, 33.

16. Theda Skocpol, "The Tocqueville Problem," *Social Science History* (winter 1997): 462.

17. Ibid., 459.

18. Ibid., 461.

19. Ibid., 467.

20. Barry Alan Shain, *The Myth of American Individualism*, 92–93.

21. Ibid., 95.

22. Ibid., xvi.

23. Rogers M. Smith, "Beyond Tocqueville, Myrdal, and Hartz: The Multiple Traditions in America," *American Political Science Review* (September 1993): 549. (Italics mine.)

24. Lee Soltow, *Distribution of Wealth and Income in the United States in 1798* (Pittsburgh: University of Pittsburgh Press, 1989), 230–231, 235–236, 237, 246.

25. Tocqueville, *Democracy in America*, 304.

26. Ibid., 513.

27. Ibid., 287.

28. Robert H. Bork, *Slouching Toward Gomorrah: Modern Liberalism and American Decline* (New York: Regan Books, 1996), 141.

29. Rogers M. Smith, "Beyond Tocqueville, Myrdal, and Hartz: The Multiple Traditions in America," *American Political Science Review*: 555.

30. Tocqueville, *Democracy in America*, 256. (Italics mine.)

31. Garry Wills, "The War Between the States . . . and Washington," *New York Times*, reprinted in *Boulder Daily Camera* (August 23, 1998): 6E.

32. Ibid.

33. Paul Hawken quoted in David C. Korten, *When Corporations Rule the World* (West Hartford, Conn.: Kumarian, and San Francisco: Berrett-Koehler, 1995), 317.

34. Ibid.

35. Tocqueville, *Democracy in America*, 614–615.

3

&

Equality and Civic Health

As I ended the previous chapter by noting the power of inequality fostered by corporate activity, I begin this chapter similarly. David Montgomery relates a potent example that rejects Tocqueville's idea that America was the stage for a growing "equality of conditions." He writes that in the first half of the nineteenth century the Chartist Thomas Ainge Devyr

> was locked in a battle on behalf of tenant farmers and wage earners on the western side of the Atlantic (America), whose ability to "govern themselves," he concluded, was jeopardized by an emerging economic system propelled by the quest for private profits within the parameters set by market forces. The more active participation in government was opened to the propertyless strata of society, the less capacity elected officials seemed to have to shape the basic contours of social life. Ray Gunn has written of the state of New York that by the 1840s "the economy was effectively insulated from democratic control."[1]

In contrast to Tocqueville's observations about America's equality, the history of the United States reveals consistent economic differences of great significance from its inception. Lee Soltow argues, "In summary, my investigations of the inequality of wealth in the United States show strong inequality in 1798, with about half of adult males having wealth. . . . Little change in economic inequality took place from 1771 to 1798 or between 1798 and 1860. . . . My working hypothesis is . . . that inequality of wealth in America remained fairly constant for the century preceding the Civil War."[2] I argue that Tocqueville's insights most commonly employed today are of worth only relative to his French homeland. As an accurate characterization of American society, they often fail to provide a realistic picture of early nineteenth century America. Thus, to employ his ideas to

today's civic virtue debate has equally misleading, and perhaps underval-
ued, implications.

To spend time refuting Tocqueville's characterization of America as a
land of equality today seems elementary, a form of child's play. Numerous studies show an increasing concentration of wealth and a leveling
off of wages and purchasing power for the average worker. These changes
produce disturbing social and political results, like the insidious control
of society by corporate interests and the cynicism and social contempt
toward institutionalized politics. Certainly, a chunk of America's social
malaise can be tied directly to the inequalities that dictate political
agendas. Yet, as I have argued, despite this cynicism and contempt, efforts to change the influence of large corporations have little success. If
Charles Lindblom's idea that business has a "privileged position" in
American politics is sound, it is also American ideology that accepts
this privileged position as essential to maintain the freedom for individual
initiative and ingenuity.[3] But a battle does exist today, because liberty
and equality appear at odds with the ability to pursue economic freedom
without restraint against the equal ability of others to exercise their basic
freedoms.

If inequality is today's elementary starting point, the more difficult task
is what do we mean when we seek greater equality? If American ideology
favors unrestrained economic activity, does the political definition of equality conflict with the ideological preference for economic freedom? In short,
will our myths about economic freedom allow us to change our economic
inequalities? To answer these questions, I will dissect Tocqueville's and
more recent theorists' insights on equality. I believe that greater economic
equality allows for greater political democracy, and thus today America
has reached perhaps its most unequal and undemocratic condition. Greater
political democracy in turn creates a strong civic culture. Despite America's
inequality, civic culture persists as citizens at their local, immediate levels
react to these pervasive inequalities. But a reactive citizen politics is not
akin to a vibrant civic culture as citizens most often lack the resources and
information to do political battle with governments and corporations that
dictate agendas. Moreover, Tocqueville's ideas on equality must be turned
upside down. He argued that America's growing equality spelled trouble
for liberty, as each citizen—being no different than any other—imposes
and is imposed by a form of subtle tyranny. I argue that economic liberty
festers to create Tocqueville's conception of negative individualism and
materialism as people are driven to distinguish themselves from their equal
neighbors. Why have individualism and materialism consumed Americans? Tocqueville thought these plagues would triumph if equality were

not tempered. I argue that these accepted characteristics of modern society triumph because equality does not exist.

FINDING TOCQUEVILLE'S POWER

Tocqueville highlights equality's potential power to undermine democracy and liberty because this social characteristic was so new and so foreign throughout history up to his era. He was concerned with equality's leveling effects—as he saw its power to constrain thought opposing majority opinion—and thus with its latent ability to overwhelm the exercise of liberty. In a society where men were roughly equal, in that property was more widely held and economic and political opportunities were greater in comparison to aristocratic Europe, he was insightful enough not to merely join democracy's bandwagon and herald its accomplishments. He worried aloud that this new form of government had elements of undoing, and democracy needed special care to succeed because of its unmitigated support. Tocqueville adds caution to America's democratic experiment, as he notes that a new, more powerful form of tyranny lies within its exercise.

Tocqueville, though, thought America quite successfully resolved this potential for tyranny through the ongoing, active civic life that buffered individuals from a potentially intrusive state. Engaged local politics, thriving with citizen interest and initiative, created a political environment that nurtured citizenship and a weak national state. Politics was not something other people did. It was not something to which professionals and bureaucrats gave their time. It remained immediate and thus important to the lives of each citizen. In a sense, Tocqueville thought equality, as democracy's latent evil, could disrupt this active, civic politics if people began to check their ideas and feelings against their equals. If their wills differed, and citizens began to hold their tongues, then conformity would rule. But conformity of thought undermines deliberation and debate; it stifles the expression of different ideas, of the ability to freely choose for oneself what one thinks and believes. In this environment, democracy falls under not a tyranny of one man rule nor a tyranny of arbitrary legal dictate. Rather, tyranny comes to the individual's mind and controls one's soul. Thus, it is not seen as arbitrarily imposed from an external power. It seeps into the citizen's thinking and determines what one advocates. To fight equality's controlling aspects, citizens need to interact. They need to practice politics as they come to define it. Through this interaction, democratic skills build and mold each into a practicing democrat.

Just as American democracy contains within it elements of its undoing,

Tocqueville notes that citizens contain within themselves characteristics that can contribute to democracy's demise. In a time of equality, if citizens become more interested in selfish pursuits to distinguish themselves from the masses, then an individualism "properly understood" does not exist. Individualism, which Tocqueville coined, was also new in its then present character, and it had the potential to destroy democracy by shifting a citizen's focus from the common good to more narrow, selfish concerns. The American propensity for industrial callings, where money and power become instant barometers of success and thus of difference from others, was one tendency Tocqueville witnessed. However, the continual, local interaction of citizens for their immediate, collective interests was pervasive. Thus, while individualism was a natural element of any freedom-loving citizen, it could be managed through collective action and expression. As Tocqueville notes, "The Americans . . . enjoy explaining almost every act of their lives on the principle of self-interest properly understood. It gives them pleasure to point out how an enlightened self-love continually leads them to help one another and disposes them freely to give part of their time and wealth for the good of the state."[4]

While individualism properly understood contributes to America's democratic health, Tocqueville is unwilling to endorse it without noting its inherent compromises. He writes:

> The doctrine of self-interest properly understood does not inspire great sacrifices, but every day it prompts some small ones; by itself it cannot make a man virtuous, but its discipline shapes a lot of orderly, temperate, moderate, careful, and self-controlled citizens. If it does not lead the will directly to virtue, it establishes habits which unconsciously turn it that way. If the doctrine of self-interest properly understood ever came to dominate all thought about morality, no doubt extraordinary virtues would be rarer. But I think gross depravity would also be rarer. Such teaching may stop some men from rising far above the common level of humanity, but many of those who fall below this standard grasp it and are restrained by it. Some individuals it lowers, but mankind it raises.[5]

This, it seems, is a utilitarian endorsement. Tocqueville recognizes individualism's power to produce democratic results, but he also recognizes its limits. Individualism properly understood does not inspire or motivate. It molds and manipulates. It is not a driving force for virtue, rather a fortunate outcome from intelligent but disparate choices. Such a qualified, perhaps in part reluctant, acceptance has pertinence for today's civic health debate. For while contemporary critics agonize over America's lack of civic virtue, it seems that Tocqueville worried over the potential for virtue even from beneficial, enlightened self-interest. Do today's critics seek virtue if it is created indirectly through intelligent self-love? When we think of virtue, do we accept that we acquire it unconsciously through habits? Should it mean more than Aristotelean practice and nurturance? Is there some standard to which we hold civic virtue, in that it sustains communal ties, traditions, and democracy itself? In short, can we accept that democracy's success is contingent upon an indirectly acquired, unconsciously formed course of action?

If so, what happens when this form of acquisition and unconscious learning are displaced by other motivations and desires? It seems that today's problem is not with equality dictating a uniform social and political agenda. America has never been more aware of its multicultural diversity, and never have these interests been reflected in public policy as well. If a tyranny of the majority does apply to American culture, it emanates from the conservative and religious factions that seek a return to some core, homogenous cultural heritage. Or, some liberals argue that corporate advertising and government platforms manufacture a tyranny of thought that precludes debate and dissension. In either or both cases, today's problem is the unexamined exercise of liberty as license, or Tocqueville's individualism wrongly understood as selfish egoism. The market economy socializes individuals to pursue selfish aims. Enlightened self-love rationalizes into the idea that private interests produce public goods. Certainly, individual moral culpability must hold citizens to some standards. But in a materialistic, bureaucratic, monied, large-scale culture, standards of morality are threatened every day not by the people. They are threatened by unenlightened behavior molded by the bottom line and motivated by the politically short term. These are the "habits of the heart" that Americans witness beyond their back yards and from their television sets.

Interestingly, though, if we jettison Tocqueville's ideas altogether—given his outdated concerns with equality rather than today's problems with liberty—we miss his important insights concerning from where inequality springs. Since his emphasis was on equality's detrimental effects, Tocqueville spent little time addressing how or from where inequality could emerge in developing America. His few comments, though, foretell Marx's and Weber's dehumanizing views about the separation between man and his labor and about the isolating effects of the division of labor. He states:

When a workman is constantly and exclusively engaged in making one object, he ends by performing this work with singular dexterity. But at the same time, he loses the general faculty of applying his mind to the way he is working. Every day he becomes more adroit and less industrious, and one may say that in his case the man is degraded as the workman improves. . . . When a workman has spent a considerable portion of his life in this fashion, his thought is permanently fixed on the object of his daily toil; his body has contracted certain fixed habits which it can never shake off. In a word, he no longer belongs to himself, but to his chosen calling. In vain are all the efforts of law and morality to break down the barriers surrounding such a man. . . . An industrial theory stronger than morality or law ties him to a trade, and often to a place, which he cannot leave.[6]

As the habits of civic involvement and enlightened self-love nurture democracy, Tocqueville notes that the habits of the division of labor undermine the development of an enlightened, whole individual. Also, and most importantly, these habits of work overwhelm any and all other habits. The necessities of industrial work form a man unable to learn democratic skills and self-government. Work's effects mold personalities, and thus present their own form of tyranny hostile to civic action and associational life. Tocqueville, then, drafts the destructive harm industrial work has on democratic self-government. Moreover, he continues:

At the same time that industrial science constantly lowers the standing of the working class, it raises that of the masters. While the workman confines his intelligence more and more to studying one single detail, the master daily embraces a vast field in his vision, and his mind expands as fast as the other's contracts. . . . So there is no resemblance between master and workman, and daily they become more different. . . . There is a constant tendency for very rich and well-educated men to devote their wealth and knowledge to manufactures. . . . Hence, just while the mass of the nation is turning toward democracy, that particular class which is engaged in industry becomes more aristocratic. . . . The industrial democracy of our day, when it has impoverished and brutalized the men it uses, abandons them in time of crisis to public charity to feed them. . . . Between workman and master there are frequent relations but no true association.[7]

Here Tocqueville describes how the structure of work separates talents and reinforces on a daily basis the divisions between these skills. While these divisions are important to produce goods, the skills of the workman, who makes up the majority of a manufacturing operation, are destructive for self-government. As the workman undergoes a detrimental transformation, the owner or capitalist learns business skills that are applicable to political activity. Because Tocqueville could not foresee the enormity and depth of industrialization on the capitalist economy, he notes that this "inequality increases within the little society (the firm or plant) in proportion as it decreases in society at large."[8] But applied to firm after firm throughout a fully industrialized capitalist economy, it seems obvious that most worker-citizens lack the democratic ability to act politically, whereas the captains of industry provide both business and political leadership. From Tocqueville's ideas, it is a logical next step to C. Wright Mills' description of a "power elite" dictating society in the 1950s and to today's revolving door syndrome as elected officials stay in Washington once their political terms conclude.[9]

At a deeper level, while not delving thoroughly into the ramifications of these insights, Tocqueville nonetheless lays out how society establishes inequality while it simultaneously embraces its causes. From his description, inequality is possible through the development of manufacturing interests. Tocqueville also argues that Americans were predisposed to pursue manufacturing interests, in that it was a method for citizens to distinguish themselves in an age of democratic equality, and it satisfied the penchant for activity and restlessness born of American equality. Thus, Tocqueville leads us to believe that human nature in a state of equality seeks to differentiate itself from its contemporaries, and in so doing, written into an age of equality is a tendency toward inequality. People seek to distinguish themselves from their neighbors, and manufactures is one possible path in an age of equal social and political status. But manufactures allows for inequality to develop, thus the condition of social and political equality motivates some to develop economic inequality, which translates easily into social and political inequalities. Tocqueville concludes his brief section on manufactures by stating, "I think that . . . the manufacturing aristocracy which we see rising before our eyes is one of the hardest that have appeared on earth. But at the same time, it is one of the most restrained and least dangerous. In any event, the friends of democracy should keep their eyes anxiously fixed in that direction. For if ever again permanent inequality of conditions and aristocracy make their way into the world, it will have been by that door that they entered."[10] Although he saw inequality to be less of a concern for democratic America than equality's leveling effects on liberty, Tocqueville gives us the source for future inequality. Although he does not conclude that inequality is a problem worth confronting, he leads us to an awareness of its potential troubles for democratic government.

From Tocqueville's insights, the immediate question worth addressing is: Given this penchant for economic individuality and thus inequality, what are the effects on social and political relations? The divisions that work fosters and the growing inequality that results, especially in today's era of employee downsizing and corporate mega-mergers, leaves workers with little connection to their work and workplace. More disturbing, as Tocqueville noted, not only do workers feel powerless from work's habits, but these attitudes carry over into other areas of life. As politics has become professionalized and more distant, and as society seeks safety in suburban enclaves quite removed from the old, inner-city neighborhood ideal, people find few possible sources of private or public attachment and interaction. Harry Boyte's free spaces, also called third spaces, defined as points of social contact for citizens to meet informally, such as bars, restaurants, churches, appear nonexistent in America's suburbs.[11] In turn, today's civic virtue debate never makes the connection that America's dismal social condition is the product of this inequality. At first created by economic inequalities that seep into social and political relations, today's railings against astronomical crime and incarceration rates, against a drugged-out culture, against teen pregnancy, against high drop-out rates, and against the welfare state are merely recognitions of social symptoms. Rather than attack the causes of these problems, it seems today's debate prefers to focus on each delinquent's lack of character and responsibility. But this seems appropriate still, if we remember that individualism properly understood never does consciously choose moral standards. It only molds and unconsciously inculcates. In an age of inequality, where differences abound, it is difficult to see how Tocqueville's properly understood individualism could arrive at an enlightened self-love of helping others in order to also help oneself. When far more examples of economic self-interest exist, the unconscious motivation turns to satisfying oneself before even thinking of anyone else. Today's deviancy is the result of individualism wrongly understood as Americans have become apologists for or unknowing adherents of economic differentiation and market freedoms. Our social condition is the consequence of persistent and thorough inequalities, those that squash individual character for most Americans, that continually reiterate the egregious differences between social classes, and that define how political activity occurs. It is to these inequalities, and their unprecedented growth in recent years, that I now turn to highlight their social and political ramifications.

ECONOMIC INEQUALITY

In terms of the rather broad category of economic inequality, research shows that America is one of, if not the, most unequal of the advanced, industrialized countries in the world. The statistics are startling. Urie Bronfenbrenner and his colleagues report that the difference between families at the 90th percentile of income, that is rich families, and those at the 10th percentile of income, or poor families, is on average $54,613, far ahead of second place Canada by over $12,000 per family.[12] Edward N. Wolff concludes that "by the 1980s the U.S. had become the most unequal industrialized country in terms of wealth. The top 1 percent of wealth holders controlled 39 percent of total household wealth in the United States in 1989, compared to 26 percent in France in 1986." Wolff continues that if he counters his critics' attacks and includes the variables he typically excludes, such as consumer goods, Social Security payments, and pensions, "the share of the richest 1 percent reached its lowest level in 1976 at 13 percent, and nearly doubled by 1989 to 22 percent."[13] Robert Reich adds more disturbing statistics. He states:

Excluding the value of homes, [the top 1 percent of families] owned 47 percent of the total household wealth of the nation. The top fifth owned 93 percent. . . . [Since 1995 when the Federal Reserve Board's] survey was completed, the stock market has surged another 30 percent annually, which suggests that wealth is even more concentrated than it was in 1995. The vast majority of Americans owned little or no stock in 1995, because they didn't have enough income to buy into the market, let alone save. According to the same Federal Reserve survey, the richest 1 percent held half of all outstanding stock and trust equity, almost two-thirds of financial securities, and more than two-thirds of business equity. The top ten-percent owned 82 percent, including indirect ownership through pensions and mutual funds. We can assume that these proportions have remained roughly the same since then, because the median wage has risen only slightly and most Americans still have little or no discretionary savings.[14]

If these numbers were not chilling enough, governmental policy of the last decade has encouraged such dismal numbers. Reich adds that, "All levels of government have shifted their sources of revenue in recent years from income taxes, property taxes, estate taxes, and taxes on capital gains (all of which tend to be progressive) to payroll taxes and taxes on sales (which tend to be regressive). As a result, the working middle class (families earning $20,000 to $50,000 a year) have been squeezed the hardest."[15] If all levels have shifted their revenue sources, this means that even the federal government, that notorious, evil bastion of unaccountable power cited by social conservatives as one of the cornerstones of today's civic corruption, is complicit in making the rich richer and the poor poorer. In short, social conservatives indict the federal government as a cause of civic decline, but certainly not when the government acts as an accomplice to the country's growing inequalities.

But before I address the federal government's role in today's civic debate, numerous other economic trends are worth noting for the disturbing and readily obvious signs of persistent and increasing inequality. In terms of working wages and a family's purchasing power, the results of the last twenty years are defeating. Bronfenbrenner and his colleagues report that, "Weekly wages [up to 1994] corrected for inflation have fallen back to levels not seen since the late 1950s."[16] Moreover, the total change in inflation-adjusted median family income has dropped 1.5% from 1973–1992, after experiencing a 55.8% increase from 1954–1973.[17] The Economic Policy Institute reinforces these findings as it discovers "the current business cycle (1989–1994) started with income declines from 1989 to 1993, the first such four-year stretch in the postwar period. Family incomes grew by $902 between 1993 and 1994, but the bottom 95% of families in 1994 still had incomes below their 1989 level, with the median family's income down 5.2%, or $2,168."[18] Holly Sklar crystallizes this data with the following checklist of figures. She states, "The combined wealth of the top 1 percent of American families is nearly the same as that of the entire bottom 95 percent. . . . Paycheck inequality has grown so much that the top 4 percent of Americans make more in wages and salaries than the entire bottom half. . . . The average CEO 'earned' as much as 41 factory workers in 1960, 42 factory workers in 1980, 104 factory workers in 1991 and 157 factory workers in 1992. . . . Between 1980 and 1993, American CEO pay increased 514 percent, workers' wages by 68 percent, consumer prices by 75 percent and corporate profits by 166 percent."[19]

In fact, an economic paradox seems to exist today, much like the confusion in the 1970s over the economy experiencing stagnation and inflation simultaneously. Economists thought it impossible then. Today, it seems difficult to ponder how gross national product can be on the rise and unemployment at record lows, at 4.5% according to August 1998 Department of Labor figures, while wages deteriorate and income growth declines. The facts indicate that economic inequality is that main culprit. Bronfenbrenner dispassionately states, "These are new and uncharted waters for the American economy. Since 1929, when the data were first collected, the United States has never before experienced a combination of a sustained rise in real GDP per capita and a persistent decline in real wages for the majority of its workforce."[20] The Economic Policy Institute adds:

We find that there seems to be no overall gain or efficiency payoff associated with all of the evident pain. There is no evidence that the economic squeeze on families is part of some sacrifice that will improve economic conditions in a way that will benefit families in the future. The economic indicators that are setting records, however, are the overall profit rate, the return of all capital income [interest, profits] per dollar of assets, and the growth of executive compensation. . . . Our review of indicators suggests that the changes in the economy have been "all pain, no gain," that the factors causing the pain of greater dislocation, economic vulnerability, and falling wages do not seem to be making a better economy or generating a "payoff" that could potentially be redistributed to help the losers. Rather, *there seems to be a large-scale redistribution of power, wealth, and income that has failed to lead to or be associated with improved economic efficiency, capital accumulation, or competitiveness.*[21]

What Tocqueville forewarned against, a new path for an aristocracy to emerge, has occurred. Christopher Lasch writes about how the elites have insulated themselves from the rest of society, sheltering themselves from the public problems that demand their participation. The conservative analyst Kevin Phillips reported first that in the 1980s "no parallel upsurge of riches had been seen since the late nineteenth century, the era of the Vanderbilts, Morgans, and Rockefellers."[22] He then continued in his next book that "America's heyday practices of the 1980s were, for the first time, those of a weakening great economic power, risking its credit and its future and abusing its middle-class citizenry for the benefit of elites and special interests."[23] The 1990s have only exacerbated those policies fostered in the 1980s, as wealth has become more concentrated and the middle-class income and wages squeezed ever tighter.

Attendant to these economic problems or economic trends, depending on your view, is a host of social consequences. But consequences is not the word most often applied. Many of today's civic virtue advocates do not see much of a relationship between economic inequality and today's social ills. Instead, they prefer to focus on America's social problems as the simplistic sign of moral decay and corruption. Bronfenbrenner and his co-authors conclude their report by claiming that "the second set of problems at the core of present-day American concerns is more difficult to characterize. Falling wages and lagging growth are well-defined phenomena; a 'decline in values' is not. . . . A seismic shift seems under way in the beliefs and values in this country, particularly those endorsed by the nations' youth. . . . Something has gone awry, many now argue, in a society in which more and more teenagers are becoming unwed mothers, in which teenagers murder teenagers with impunity, in which civility, community, and safety are fast disappearing in many urban areas."[24] It seems that the deteriorating economic conditions that these authors cite as the first set of problems at America's core have no effect on America's second set of problems. As Ben J. Wattenberg adds, "I have come to the conclusion that the values issues are no longer merely co-equal with economic concerns. The values issues are now the most important."[25] The values issues such as teen pregnancy, welfare dependency, and the breakdown of the traditional family strike at the root of society, but from a different voice these problems are reflective of, not independent from, America's changing economic condition.

Let us take one of the most poignant statistics that strikes at the heartstrings of all Americans. Close to 25 percent of all American children live in poverty, as do 20.4% of children under the age of eighteen. This latter statistic is more than twice the rate of any other advanced country in the world.[26] Social conservatives emphasize that these statistics are the result of unwed teens giving birth. In turn, their resulting lack of job opportunities, due to dropping out of school to care for their children, perpetuate welfare dependency and a cycle of lost opportunities and training. Children born into poverty find it difficult to escape it themselves, and the cycle of lost opportunity spins through generations. Only a stronger moral code and a tighter family structure with a tougher means-tested access to stringent benefits can provide a tough-love remedy to this cycle of poverty, poor education, and dependency. The civic virtue of this class is nonexistent because of their dependency on the system. They cannot contribute to the collective good.

As a counter argument to every topic in this common and divisive analysis, David M. Gordon indicates the economic causes and the inherent misguided beliefs that perpetuate dependency instead of resolving it. He claims:

Name the problem—the "family breakdown," "welfare dependency," "teen pregnancy"—and . . . we can find falling real wages or job insecurity lurking in the background as a primary contributing cause of that problem. The corporate production system, and the kinds of jobs it provides or fails to provide, hold the key to understanding much of what we currently debate. . . . In seeking to understand the stresses . . . on Americans' lives and communities, rather than spend so much time blaming deviants or moral pestilents we should focus . . . on the character of employment in the United States.[27]

Gordon then proceeds to examine each issue. The breakdown of the family, he argues, may have destructive social consequences, unless, of course, you are a woman dependent on an intolerant or abusive husband for your, and especially for your children's, care. Gordon cites Elaine McCrate's research that uncovers a direct relationship between women's economic independence and the decline in marriage. According to her results, economic reasons for marriage become less a motivating factor in women's lives when they have the opportunities to support themselves.[28] Gordon says that because of the wage and income squeeze that male bread-holders have experienced over the last twenty-five years, men offer women fewer reasons to stay in difficult marriages, or in general to enter them in the first place. Not that women's wages have risen significantly or even match men's salaries, but greater opportunities exist for women today than a generation or two ago. If escaping a difficult marriage and an oppressive environment for children, then the breakdown of the traditional family seems a social good, rather than a social ill.

About teen pregnancy, Gordon cites the 1993 Statistical Abstract that today's debate over teenage pregnancy is wholly misleading. Teenage pregnancy, in fact, has decreased significantly over the last twenty years. It is less of a social concern, meaning that fewer teenage women become pregnant than in 1970. In that year, roughly 16 percent of mothers were teenagers. In 1990, the figure decreased to about 12 percent. Even in absolute numbers, the levels have decreased. In light of these facts, the national discussion adds unwarranted hysteria to a social condition that is undergoing significant change.[29] Gordon then questions conventional wisdom and argues that teenage mothers in fact may go ahead with childbearing given their low adult earnings expectations. Again, McCrate's research in this field reveals the lack of any positive relationship between being a teenage mother and future earnings potential. At first blush, this non-relationship seems counter-intuitive. Certainly, the additional demands of caring for children must impinge on the mother's ability to earn an education and find decent employment. However, the research shows that higher education has little effect on earnings power, especially for African-American teenage mothers. Of additional concern, expectations of earning power has a strong influence on teenage motherhood. If teenagers sense that additional education will have little effect on their ability to find meaningful employment, whether from friends' or families' experiences or from the general lack of opportunities in their surroundings, then motherhood is quite likely.[30] The conclusion, then, is that teen pregnancy has become a more distressful result primarily because adequate jobs do not exist for the working mothers who must care for their children. Morality is no longer the issue, or rather, the main issue. Instead, a sustainable economy that provides employment opportunities becomes the public policy focus.

Welfare dependency gets similar treatment. Most of the rationalizations for why the 1990s economy grows as most of its workers suffer focuses on several myths, one of which is the skills or technology mismatch thesis. The argument runs that those without the proper education, tools, and training fail to advance because their skills do not meet the new technologies that the growing economy needs. However, the Economic Policy Institute counters, "The basic portrait of wage shifts does not easily fit a technology/skill explanation. First, we have already noted that the groups experiencing wage losses are not a small group readily labeled 'unskilled,' since in the 1990s those for whom wages fell included the bottom 80% of men and the bottom 60% of women. Many of the workers have high school degrees, if not two-year or four-year college degrees. . . . Second, since the mid-1980s wage inequality has taken the form of the top tier of earners pulling away from both middle- and low-wage earners to an equal degree."[31] This response to the skills mismatch thesis focuses on the pain that most all workers have experienced over the course of this decade. At the other extreme, Gordon cites the misleading myths that surround AFDC recipients. Only a quarter of these recipients rely solely on this funding, whereas the other 75 percent combine AFDC payments with outside, and usually unreported, work with family contributions. He reiterates a common theme in the urban underclass field of study—that the job opportunities are so abysmal that women with children working full time could never earn enough money to reach the official government poverty levels, levels many critics cite as wholly inadequate to support a family.[32] While the 1990s economy produces high-tech jobs, it also produces significantly more minimum wage jobs that cannot possibly sustain any family for any length of time without some outside source of support.

While Gordon diverts the understanding of our social problems back to our elemental economic policies and employment decisions, Verba, Schlozman, and Brady focus on the civic or political consequences of America's economic inequality. Their conclusions that the wealthy dominate political activity, especially since political activity has turned from volunteering time to donating money, and thus influence public policy, should come as little surprise. Certainly, those who participate in politics sing a different tune in a different key than those who do not. The authors state "the disadvantaged are more than twice as likely . . . to discuss concerns about basic human needs such as poverty, jobs, housing, and health. In contrast, the activity of the advantaged . . . is more likely to have been inspired by economic issues such as taxes, government spending, or the budget, or by social issues such as abortion or pornography."[33] The conclusions for America's civic health, then, appear obvious. If the growing economic inequalities influence who is heard by, and thus the policies proposed by our elected officials, then America quickly turns into an economy and a polity "insulated from democratic control." Our civic health, then, results from our moral condition, and our moral condition is indelibly linked to our economic trends. As Verba, Schlozman, and Brady conclude, "Political conflict in America has traditionally been less deeply imbued with the rhetoric of class than in other democracies. . . . Nevertheless, when it comes to political participation, class matters profoundly for American politics. As long as inequalities in education and income persist, as long as Americans have unequal opportunities to develop and practice civic skills, and as long as citizens increasingly donate money rather than time to politics, the voices heard through the medium of citizen participation will be loud, clear, and far from equal."[34]

If economic inequality calls political democracy into question, the federal government is also complicit in creating an ineffective democratic politics. Social conservatives claim that the government's size is the main problem, as its distance at the federal level and unaccountable largesse in social programs promote a culture of irresponsibility. However, size may not be the principal problem. Instead, certain political agendas and confusing information cloud the information available for citizens. Sklar argues that almost any measure of economic status or trends should be questioned because of their inaccuracies, whether political or not. She cites:

The government has not adjusted the poverty formula to reflect the current cost of food, which is now much lower in relation to housing, health care and other necessities, such as child care for working parents. It simply takes the previous year's poverty line, based on an increasingly inadequate formula, and adjusts it for inflation. . . . In their book on the working poor, John Schwarz and Thomas Volgy show that a family of four needed an income of about 155 percent of the official poverty line to buy minimally sufficient food, housing, health care, transportation, clothing and other personal and household items, and pay taxes. . . . Using Schwarz and Volgy's formula, one person in four is living in poverty. By contrast, the official 1993 poverty rate was 15 percent.[35]

Unemployment statistics are another example. The official unemployment rates include only those who have looked for work within the last three weeks. It does not include those who are part-time but seek full-time employment, those who are underemployed, or those who simply have stopped looking. Lester Thurow concludes, "Properly calculated, our rate of joblessness is well into double digits. No wonder workers have no bargaining power to get their share of an increasingly productive economy."[36] The reason why workers lack bargaining power is due to millions of workers who are underemployed in part-time or "independent contracting" work, which exerts little pressure on companies to increase wages. In fact, a common view is that these independent contractors scramble for work they are lucky to get. Thurow adds that a more accurate figure for unemployment and underemployment is over 25% of the workforce, as about half of this figure comes from the "8.1 million American workers in temporary jobs, 2 million who work 'on call,' and 8.3 self-employed 'independent contractors' [many of whom are downsized professionals who have very few clients but call themselves self-employed consultants because they are too proud to admit that they are unemployed]. . . . In the words of *Fortune* magazine, 'Upward pressure on wages is nil because so many of the employed are these contingent workers who have no bargaining power with employers, and payroll workers realize they must swim in the same Darwinian ocean.'"[37]

While government statistics are misleading, and thus allow politicians and corporations to allude social analysis and revision, the Federal Reserve Board, as an unchecked component of the federal government, also fails to address these fundamental inequalities. Actually, the Fed contributes to these inequalities. James K. Galbraith argues that the Fed remains wedded to controlling inflation, and thereby promoting policies that limit economic growth at or below 2.5% per year. Anything above this is considered inflationary. However, Thurow views the war on inflation as not only victorious, but as having produced detrimental overkill. He states, "Like a real war that has gone on far too long, all of the original reasons for the war—the mis-financing of the Vietnam War, OPEC oil shocks, food shocks, indexed wage and supply contracts, inflationary expectations— are long gone. As the war continues year after year, the negative side effects of the war, falling real wages and rising inequalities, have become far more corrosive than the original reasons for joining the battle."[38] In addition to those causes cited by Thurow, what is one of the main forces that supposedly drives inflation upward? An increase in wages, and so the pernicious decline in real wages and income in general for the vast majority of Americans is a well-defined Fed strategy encompassing the last ten to twenty years. Galbraith adds, "The old relationship between inflation and labor costs really has busted up since Reagan fired the air traffic controllers and he and Volcker overvalued the dollar. Prices may be rising at 2.7 percent annually, but real wages are scarcely moving. Indeed we find that all inflation accelerations after 1960, with the sole exception of that following Richard Nixon's election campaign in 1972, were led by prices and not by wages."[39]

To rail against government solely is to view only one aspect of our social condition. Gordon believes corporate America employs a basic strategy that dramatically hurts workers' lives. Gordon calls it the 'Stick Strategy' in that corporations have little interest in using a carrot approach. He argues despite the common understanding that the 1990s have witnessed a profound downsizing in corporate employment, America's corporations are still top-heavy with middle and upper management. The production line has felt the downsizing squeeze most, as firms have left American towns for overseas markets to find rock-bottom labor costs. In fact, Gordon believes that since workers have been downsized, the result is that the proportion of managerial positions in relation to overall job categories has increased in the 1990s, as more managers are necessary to control the remaining workers who may feel increasingly hostile in an uncaring corporate environment. Thus, he believes this growing managerial top-heaviness increases the bureaucracy and administration of corporate America.[40] In addition to this bureaucratic burden, corporate America has used the well-documented wage freeze or wage squeeze to stifle employees' voices. He concludes that both are used in conjunction with the other, as each depends on the other. He states:

> In one direction, stagnant or falling wages create the need for intensive managerial supervision of frontline employees. If workers do not share in the fruits of the enterprise . . . what incentive do they have to work as hard as their bosses would like? So the corporations need to monitor the workers' effort and be able to threaten credibly to punish them if they do not perform. The corporations must wield the Stick. Eventually the Stick requires millions of Stick-wielders.
>
> In the other direction, once top-heavy corporate bureaucracies emerge, they acquire their own . . . expansionary dynamic. They push for more numbers in their ranks and higher salaries for their members. Where does the money come from? . . . One of the most obvious targets is frontline workers' compensation. The more powerful the corporate bureaucracy becomes, and the weaker the pressure with which employees can counter, the greater the downward pressure on production workers' wages. The wage squeeze intensifies.[41]

As statistics show, and as researchers continue to argue, today there is very little pressure on corporate America for higher wages. The wage squeeze strategy has worked as increasingly more employees are in temporary or underemployed work categories, and without the heavy costs of health benefits and compensation plans. In fact, the General Motors strike in the summer of 1998 was viewed by some economists as having a beneficial effect not for employees' wages and power, but rather for cooling an overheated, highly productive economy.[42] It seems that economic inequality is a corporate strategy, fueled by either ineffective or complicit governmental action, that guarantees dire social and political consequences. In fact, today's civic health debate can be seen as a chink in the corporate strategy, in that its mere discussion allows for a heated debate about its origins. But given the success of what Gordon calls a corporate strategy that is both fat and mean, and the ability of social conservatives to direct the civic virtue debate, it seems economics will remain a minor issue in what has become a divisive cultural war. And as Thurow argues, yet another war not worth fighting anymore.

DEFINING EQUALITY

If economic inequality is the pervasive sign of our times, then what does any change seek to accomplish? More specifically, what do I mean when I argue for greater equality? Much like the term *civic virtue*, equality means far different things depending on the perspective. Also, any significant change in today's understanding confronts the power of tradition and myth that give weighty meaning to people's ideologies—ideologies both simple and complex. In turn, these forces establish and entrench values, even if these values appear irrelevant to the changing times. In general, though, America today sees equal opportunity as the defining characteristic of equality, but affirmative action, quotas, and a host of other preferential justifications modify simple opportunity. These programs come under attack because not only do they change equality's definition, but they also necessitate the government's role as enforcer of a disputed collective will. Today's attack on inequality, then, often spurs a counterattack on the government's intrusion on freedom. This centuries old duality points to the difficulty in reconciling equality with liberty and in satisfying the general good while also allowing individual preferences and creativity to flourish.

It seems a universal dictum today that a certain degree of inequality is preferable to significant constraints on liberty. The belief is that social and economic inequality are more transient, or transformable, characteristics in comparison to limits on freedom. In a sense, the traditional theoretical understanding is that from liberty springs the social and economic opportunities to satisfy their unequal distribution. As America has proven, whereas political liberty demands a threshold between freedom and nonfreedom, greater variability exists—in a sense the threshold is more amorphous and changeable—for social and economic equalities. Liberty is a necessary condition for equality, as it seems unlikely to ever have a polity with truly equal and empowered citizens who also lack political freedom. For instance, totalitarian regimes restrict liberty and grant equality in name only, as citizens are never equal socially, politically, or economically. If liberty is necessary for (in)equality, today's theoretical conclusion is that exacting equality is not necessary for liberty. In democratic America especially, a consensus recognizes that freedom spawns differences, and those differences create inequalities that must be acknowledged and safeguarded. However, also in America, a history of research shows the stifling effects on liberty by any concentration of inequality. For instance, public policy is the reflection of who votes, and since the poor do not have the same economic resources as the wealthy, their powerlessness leads to political nonrepresentation. The same held true for the elderly thirty to forty years ago until they were organized politically; now it holds true for children, the underclasses, and very broadly minorities.

Tocqueville thought that America successfully resolved the tension between liberty and equality in a democratic society beholden to individual rights by employing three principal mechanisms. First, Americans displayed an enlightened individualism that fueled initiative and opportunity along with a concern for the general welfare. Given that America was a smaller, perhaps more tradition-bound place at the time—and just about to embark on its individualistic form of capitalist growth—the concern for the public will was more obvious and immediate to its citizens. Second, Tocqueville saw this enlightened individualism in practice when he witnessed the numerous associational groups Americans created. This penchant for joining together to solve public problems provided a strong buffer against the intrusions of the state—a state at that time that was rather meager and without many functions. Finally, and most importantly, Tocqueville recognized the role of customs, habits, and mores that influenced individual behavior and guided the public weal. It is these habits that have more power to determine individual and collective behavior than any force of law or any group proclamation. Along with tradition, Tocqueville saw religion as a moderating force in changing times. In the Burkean tradition, religion provides sustenance and meaning for proper, public-spirited action from individuals. However, as for equality, Tocqueville's ideas are hardly a recasting of Burke's conservative agenda. Steven DeLue states:

> The individual in Tocqueville's society locates him- or herself in traditions and habits that sustain equality, the equality that is necessary to maintain for people their personal freedom and rights. Unlike Burke, the Tocquevillean individual would be suspicious of natural forms of social order that place people into various roles and that permit an elite to rule. . . . But for Tocqueville, equality is best manifested in settings that permit individuals to take part in the ongoing activities of group and local government life and in the forming of group and local government objectives and goals. . . . These individuals, by virtue of being able to help formulate solutions to common problems in local government settings, would be fiercely independent people, who do not look for government to take care of them.[43]

With this emphasis on equality's importance in sustaining personal freedom and the need for engaged citizen input in solving public issues, Tocqueville's views are hard to typecast today as a purely conservative philosophy. Though, civic virtues to create a moderate, disciplined individual resistant to material excess and bound by the power of tradition and obligation resonate strongly with conservative ideas. But such views also resonate with liberal thinkers. The difference between today's conservative agenda and the liberal response is that conservatives concentrate on Tocqueville's view of civic virtue and morality while they do not recognize the importance of the market's influence on this morality. Liberals want to secure individualism and its vibrancy through the guarantee of rights, and it is sometimes these rights that dissolve tradition and the notion of some predetermined, and perhaps individually oppressive, morality. Essentially in Tocqueville's ideas are the elements to continue the tension between equality and liberty.

Because moderating economic inequality seems a daunting social and political task, fighting Sisyphean battles against both anti-government ideology and pro-market freedoms, Mickey Kaus argues that democracy's demise today comes from its lack of social equality rather than just economic inequality. As the wealthy insulate themselves from the deteriorating public sphere, there is less social interaction in general and less class intermingling in particular. To have more viable public spaces requires an interest from all segments of society, and especially from the class that has the greatest ability to pay for it. More importantly, though, the necessary interaction public places demand creates a sense of solidarity that unites a community. Instead of bunkering in manicured, gated communities, the interaction of the most well-off with those of other classes maintains the customs and traditions that Tocqueville considers essential to a well-guided population. In a tougher next step, Christopher Lasch seeks to push Kaus's argument further. Lasch claims that "economic inequality is intrinsically undesirable, even when confined to it proper sphere. Luxury is morally repugnant, and its incompatibility with democratic ideals, moreover, has been consistently recognized in the traditions that shape our political culture. The difficulty of limiting the influence of wealth suggests that wealth itself needs to be limited."[44] I think it important to add that no bastion of public excellence, no creation of public spaces that produce profound joy, enthusiasm, and pride in the population can replace the poverty an individual endures. This seems so because of America's firm grasp on individualism, and the Tocquevillean notion of "forever being thrown back upon oneself alone."[45] Perhaps if American culture focused more on the general good, much like many European nations, then economic inequalities would produce fewer social and political ills. However, in America poverty simply does not let people enjoy public treasures as well as they should. For example, what are today's public spaces to which the public flocks for recreation, leisure, and family time? The shopping mall, and while it grows bigger in size and services, it also ironically displays the vast differences between those who come to the mall for the experience itself and those who shop at its exclusive stores.[46]

Moreover, it is foolish to think that strong, vibrant public spaces can replace the problems that fundamental economic inequalities produce. Only when wealth and money do not have the ability to influence areas outside of the marketplace can we begin to think political democracy can accommodate vast economic inequalities. In essence, Michael Walzer argues for this approach in that no one individual, corporation, or even class can dominate social goods. This is not to say that these goods are not monopolized, only that "no particular good is generally convertible. . . . Though there will be many small inequalities, inequality will not be multiplied through the conversion process. . . . And the resistance to convertibility would be maintained, in large degree, by ordinary men and women within their own spheres of competence and control, without large-scale state action."[47] Yet, without large-scale state action, and sometimes with it, economic inequalities increase exponentially. What are the common views of society and politics today? Money buys power, and money buys access. Add to these that money buys fame, beauty, and admiration, and Tocqueville was only half right when he wrote that in an age of equality, money becomes the barometer of difference. Why he was only half right is because we no longer live in an age of equality. By equality, Tocqueville meant that the population had similar ideas about what is important and that all roughly adhered to what all others sought. But when vast inequality underlies society, as Verba, Schlozman, and Brady report, different segments of the population focus on and worry about different public goods.

Still, is it clearer what *equality* must mean today? Thomas Nagel states, "It does not seem plausible to defend the wealth of a few in perfectionist terms drawn from the example of social support for the artistic or scientific or scholarly work of a few, or for the preservation of the natural order. These latter perfectionist goals are legitimate collective ends because their unequal benefits to individuals is incidental. But wealth is primarily a benefit to individuals, and therefore subject to egalitarian constraints."[48] From Nagel's words, one central issue of democracy boils down to the effects of wealth on other members of the collectivity and what the collectivity considers a legitimate degree of wealth that does not adversely affect what they determine justice to be. It seems the one certainty within this definitional ambiguity is that for a democracy to function, citizens must be capable of expressing their different ideas. When economic rewards limit this function, then either the democracy needs redefinition or citizens must exert their collective power to claim their legitimate control. David Held defines the democratic tension between equality and liberty with his concept of democratic autonomy. He states, "The model of democratic autonomy is to enhance the choices and benefits which flow from living in a society that does not leave large categories of citizens in a permanently subordinate position, at the mercy of forces entirely outside their control. . . . It is going to be a matter for citizens themselves to decide, within the framework set down by the principle of autonomy, how exactly goods and services are to be distributed."[49] Again, the phrases 'permanently subordinate position' and 'forces entirely outside their control' provide more uncertainty than clarity when choices must be made. The underlying fact, consistent with the other theorists' ideas, is that the Tocquevillean notion of ongoing citizen input and interaction is mandatory for democracy. From these theoretical overlaps, and viewing the data on the inequality of democratic participation fostered by economic conditions, the necessary beginning for a more legitimate American democratic state starts with the decrease in the influence of money throughout the political system and the guarantee of the inclusion of those whom the collectivity views as subordinate.

This is certainly not enough, and certainly open to question. While I have examined Tocqueville's conservative theoretical aspects, today conservatives dominate the debate about civic virtue. They invoke a sense of lost morality and a decline in civic interaction—those conservative aspects of Tocqueville's philosophy he thought most crucial for democracy's survival. Why liberals seem either lost or silent in this debate is because they are uneasy around notions of collective morality. Rather, the liberal persuasion emphasizes the protection of individual rights against either an intrusive state, some moral majority, or simply the idea of popular rule. While they certainly recognize and agree that society only succeeds democratically with a collective morality, to call for a return to a specific moral era or to call for certain tenents of conduct smacks of intolerance and a lack of respect for others. Also, while they emphasize economic differences as the cause for social and political inequalities and the destruction of civic virtue, as I do here, they also recognize that economic differences can exist and yet be moderated somewhat by a strong civic commitment. It was possible for America to exhibit both a degree of significant inequality and yet display local civic and political interaction in the early nineteenth century. That is what Tocqueville witnessed. However, today those inequalities are so profound that they determine civic and political interaction to a significantly detrimental degree. Thus, these inequalities demand immediate attention. Civic virtue is dependent upon more than just economic conditions, but when economic conditions affect nearly all private and public relations, then their public assessment is vital to democracy's health.

To assume that only conservatives dictate the social debate about civic life undervalues John Rawls' theory of justice. Rawls pursues a liberal formula of securing first specific rights for individuals. From the universal "original position" in choosing how to adopt the principles of justice, individuals under a "veil of ignorance" about their specific futures would decide that the principal goods of society would be distributed according to the following guidelines:

First: each person is to have an equal right to the most extensive basic liberty compatible with a similar liberty for others. Second: social and economic inequalities are to be arranged so that they are both (a) to the greatest benefit of the least advantaged, and (b) attached to positions and offices open to all under conditions of fair equality of opportunity.[50]

The first condition guarantees what we commonly view as a rights-based liberalism, well-recognized in American society today. These include the right to vote and run for office, and the freedoms associated with the Bill of Rights. The second condition, though, runs radically against how America conducts itself today. For while America seeks to establish equal opportunities for all to compete for various jobs and goods—in fact this is the argument against affirmative action today—the forces of tradition, power, and money undermine any notion of fairness. In response, the idea of the least advantaged receiving, for example, some of the better-offs' wealth is anathema in America. For while Rawls sees this condition as necessary to maintain equality and self-respect, in a sense for an individual to remain a viable participant in the democratic polity, critics argue that redistributing wealth and other rewards that arise from initiative inhibits freedom and the beneficial products of creativity and plain, hard work. For Rawls, inequalities form given the natural differences in talent and creativity that people express, but in order for all to flourish, these inequalities must be muted to some extent to allow all to have the opportunities to express themselves. He continues that his rights-based approach is essential because it allows for an "overlapping consensus" from the disparate segments of society. Some may not agree to certain societal principles, but all can agree on the rights accorded to each citizen. It is from this consensus that civic society sustains the polity, for the consensus establishes agreement on fundamental tenents, and civic society initiates actions to uphold these tenents. These actions include public education, the belief that the state will interfere only minimally, if at all, in the actions of the civic groups and in individuals' lives, and that citizens have the opportunity to participate in stating their ideas and even their moral opinions.

As with the several other theories briefly explored, Rawls' ideas overlap in a few areas. Although it is unlikely to see America redistributing wealth as radically as Rawls' ideas demand, the important theoretical similarity lies in the ability of individuals to select without constraint how they choose to live. But more importantly for democracy, it is through citizen action and interaction that these choices exist. Certainly, as conservatives emphasize, guideposts for action and choice must be established. These are the forces of tradition and custom that Tocqueville heralds. However, if truly democratic, these guideposts of tradition also must be reassessed through citizen involvement. Founding principles such as free speech and the free practice of religion provide lasting structure while law and traditions are open to debate and revision.

Just how far away is America from Rawls' formula for enacting equality and justice? While the power of corporate America appears at its zenith these days, there exists a small measure of disquietude toward its influence and practices. If, in fact, corporate wealth and elite mobility increasingly come into question, then perhaps the myths that surround their power will tumble and create greater opportunities for the start of a public examination of what constitutes justice and equality today. As a sign of this minor undercurrent, Robert Reich writes:

America can afford to do more, because the rich have grown breathlessly wealthier, and they can afford to do more. A progressive tax on wealth should not be beyond imagination. . . . And no one would get soaked; this isn't a zero-sum game in which the rich lose and the middle and below win. A better-educated and healthier society is in everyone's interest. Tie a progressive wealth tax to tax cuts for middle- and lower-income earners, to an education trust fund to rebuild schools and attract the very best talent to teaching, to universal health care. Perhaps consider a "grubstake" of $25,000 for every young person who finishes high school, to be spent on additional education or invested. The public would get a twofer: an incentive for young people to finish high school, and a whole new generation of capitalists.[51]

Reich's recommendations sound much like Rawls' radicalism. Moving from individuals to corporations, Paul Kalra adds that controlling multinationals might include "the replacement of the corporate income tax with a Value Added Tax (VAT) and the taxation of corporate earnings through individual stockholders independent of how and where they are reinvested. Lester C. Thurow . . . has suggested that a 14 percent VAT would raise enough revenue to replace the corporate and payroll taxes. . . . VATs between 15 and 25 percent are common in western Europe. . . . One advantage of VAT over the corporate income tax is that it is free of loopholes and less subject to manipulation by the multinationals."[52] Finally, Lasch argues that economic change is necessary for the very reason that conservatives argue civic culture needs to change. At base, equality is both a political and moral component of society. He states, "When money talks, everybody else is condemned to listen. For that reason a democratic society cannot allow unlimited accumulation. Social and political equality presuppose at least a rough approximation of economic equality. . . . [W]e . . . need to remember that boundaries are permeable, especially where money is concerned, that a moral condemnation of great wealth must inform any defense of the free market, and that moral condemnation must be backed up with effective political action."[53]

At last, then, does a more acute definition of equality within democratic confines emerge? It seems that equality in America battles endlessly with the power of individualism and its modern preference for unrestricted freedom. This is the individualism Tocqueville feared, as its unenlightened view dismisses the connection between individual behavior and the common good. Perhaps economic conditions do not constitute the sole factor in social and political relations as Marx thought, but economic inequalities foster constraints that dictate how democracy functions. Today's unenlightened view of equality, then, ironically opens up at best the possibility for an appraisal of democratic principles and justice. When those fundamental questions exist, social and political action will likely assert control over economic injustices. I argue these fundamental questions exist today, and America's civic health debate is merely one aspect—perhaps a misguided aspect at that—of a roiling social current that demands public attention.

NOTES

1. David Montgomery, *Citizen Worker: The Experience of Workers in the United States with Democracy and the Free Market during the Nineteenth Century* (New York: Cambridge University Press, 1993), 2.

2. Lee Soltow, *Distribution of Wealth and Income in the United States in 1798* (Pittsburgh: University of Pittsburgh Press, 1989), 243.

3. Charles E. Lindblom, *Politics and Markets: The World's Political-Economic Systems* (New York: Basic Books, 1977), 170–188.

4. Alexis de Tocqueville, *Democracy in America*, ed. J. P. Mayer (New York: HarperPerennial, 1969), 526.

5. Ibid., 527.

6. Ibid., 555–556.

7. Ibid., 556–558.

8. Ibid., 556–557.

9. C. Wright Mills, *The Power Elite* (New York: Oxford University Press, 1956).

10. Alexis de Tocqueville, *Democracy in America*, 558.

11. Harry C. Boyte, *The Backyard Revolution: Understanding the New Citizen Movement* (Philadelphia: Temple University Press, 1980), 24, 36–43.

12. Urie Bronfenbrenner, Peter McClelland, Elaine Wethington, Phyllis Moen, and Stephen J. Ceci, *The State of Americans: This Generation and the Next* (New York: The Free Press, 1996), 149.

13. Edward N. Wolff, "How the Pie Is Sliced," *The American Prospect*, no. 22 (summer 1995): 60–61.

14. Robert B. Reich, "My Dinner with Bill," *The American Prospect*, no. 38 (May–June 1998): 9.

15. Ibid.

16. Urie Bronfenbrenner, et al., *The State of Americans*, 57.

17. Ibid., 58.

18. Economic Policy Institute, "The State of Working America 1996–1997," (Washington, D.C.: Economic Policy Institute, 1996) (http://epn.org/epi/epswa-in.html), 3.

19. Holly Sklar, *Chaos or Community?: Seeking Solutions, Not Scapegoats for Bad Economics* (Boston: South End Press, 1995), 5, 8–9.

20. Urie Bronfenbrenner, et al., 64.

21. Economic Policy Institute, "The State of Working America 1996–1997," 2, 6.

22. Kevin Phillips, *The Politics of Rich and Poor: Wealth and the American Electorate in the Reagan Aftermath* (New York: Random House, 1990), 10.

23. Kevin Phillips, *Boiling Point: Republicans, Democrats and the Decline of Middle-Class Prosperity* (New York: HarperPerennial, 1994), 36.

24. Urie Bronfenbrenner, et al., 260.

25. Ben J. Wattenberg, *Values Matter Most: How Republicans or Democrats or a Third Party Can Win and Renew the American Way of Life* (New York: The Free Press, 1995), 13.

26. Urie Bronfenbrenner, et al., 148.

27. David M. Gordon, *Fat and Mean: The Corporate Squeeze of Working Americans and the Myth of Managerial 'Downsizing'* (New York: The Free Press, 1996), 115.

28. Ibid., 119.

29. Ibid., 123–124.

30. Ibid., 124–125.

31. Economic Policy Institute, 15.

32. David M. Gordon, 126.

33. Sidney Verba, Kay Lehman Schlozman, and Henry E. Brady, "The Big Tilt: Participatory Inequality in America," *The American Prospect*, no. 32 (May–June 1997): 78.

34. Ibid., 80.

35. Holly Sklar, *Chaos or Community?*, 11–13.

36. Lester Thurow, "The Crusade That's Killing Prosperity," *The American Prospect*, no. 25 (March–April 1996): 54.

37. Ibid., 56.

38. Ibid., 55.

39. James K. Galbraith, "The Surrender of Economic Policy," *The American Prospect*, no. 25 (March–April 1996): 62–63.

40. David M. Gordon, *Fat and Mean*, 5.

41. Ibid., 5-6.

42. Michael Hirsh, "Is This Strike to Like?," *Newsweek* (July 13, 1998): 46.

43. Steven M. DeLue, *Political Thinking, Political Theory, and Civil Society* (Boston: Allyn and Bacon, 1997), 248.

44. Christopher Lasch, *The Revolt of the Elites and the Betrayal of Democracy* (New York: W. W. Norton and Company, 1995), 22.

45. Alexis de Tocqueville, *Democracy in America*, 508.

46. Today's shopping mall epitomizes America's pervasive inequality and the meager attempts to resolve it. For while the mall retains its public dimension, in that anyone can walk its hallways and observe its social functions, many of the mall's visitors find themselves economically excluded from many, if not most, of its stores. In a sense, then, the poor remain only passive social observers; they are physically limited by their lack of buying power to participate in the principal activity of the mall's existence. Perhaps for Kaus, malls may be a civic space worth cultivating, but the fundamental difference in this environment is economic and not social. Ultimately, any social dimension at a mall exists in the context of purchasing. Moreover, emotionally the poor fall victim to Tocqueville's idea that in times of equality, people consume themselves with an eye toward their neighbors and what their neighbors possess. The poor, as Tocqueville notes about the "workman," suffer not just in their pocket but also in their public perception and self-conscious public review. They are considered as somehow less of people because wealth is one of today's foremost personal values. In the end, for politics, the ability to only "window-shop" undermines democracy's health. To carry this analogy even further, today we see the newest malls as exclusively catering to a rich clientele, with even the anchor stores trying to move into the crowded market for the upscale dollar. A mall often does have a store for all of society's classes, but the distinction between them is dramatic. Furthermore, the simple matter of going to the mall excludes many poor, and thus highlights the distinction of wealth starting only from a middle-class perspective.

47. Michael Walzer, *Spheres of Justice: A Defense of Pluralism and Equality* (New York: Basic Books, 1983), 17.

48. Thomas Nagel, *Equality and Partiality* (New York: Oxford University Press, 1991), 137–138.

49. David Held, *Models of Democracy*, 2nd ed. (Stanford: Stanford University Press, 1996), 331.

50. John Rawls, *A Theory of Justice* (Cambridge: Harvard University Press, 1971), 60, 83.

51. Robert B. Reich, "My Dinner with Bill," *The American Prospect*, no. 38, 9.

52. Paul Kalra, *The American Class System: Divide and Rule* (Pleasant Hill, CA: Antenna Publishing Co., 1995), 151.

53. Christopher Lasch, *The Revolt of the Elites*, 22.

4

∽

Confronting Complexity

My argument thus far is straightforward. As a basis for today's civic health discussion, Tocqueville's ideas are double-edged. His observations are biased by an aristocratic, state-centralized heritage that allows him to view America, with its lack of privileged status and very rough economic and political opportunities, as a watershed for democratic society. It is dubious, however, to assume that America ever truly experienced the "equality of conditions" that Tocqueville described. Wealth has always been distributed vastly unequally; the point is whether this inequality merits collective action because of its social and political effects. The idea of protected individual rights provides some buffer against the intrusion of money on democracy's health. Also, after the Depression, the public outcry that produced a government interested in welfare politics again attempts to counter the ill effects of lasting and profound wealth. Both changes, though, while revolutionary in their day, today pass as a façade of control, as an apparent check that lacks substance against inequality. Rather, what comes to the forefront of today's debate is Tocqueville's understanding of the civic value of associational life, where individual Americans were quick and motivated to join with their neighbors to create and satisfy public goods. In early America, Tocqueville tells us, individuals understood that rights came only with the good.

Thus, Tocqueville may have been correct if by *equality of conditions* he meant Americans had reached a social contract about a few fundamental views. Perhaps Americans recognized the importance of individuals acting for collective ends, the importance of sharing similar ideas about what constitutes a productive, healthy life, and the importance of active, ongoing involvement. These shared views do not exist today, and the present condition has every political scribe calling for a return to a more civil society with a more civic outlook. A civic outlook generates initiative that excludes government's labyrinth. It informs as it teaches democratic skills. It fosters the traditions and customs that gird democracy from disintegration. These calls, though, often lack the essential democratic elements of toleration and mutual respect. For while they rail against family disintegration, welfare dependency, drug abuse, and crime, they fail to notice the independence and inclusion that the last forty years of social changes foster. Women's independence, they claim, comes at the cost of wayward children. Welfare creates leeches and not self-supporters. Selfishness guides behavior, with no concern for public concerns. More importantly, these calls for a civic revivalism demand only that individuals change their destructive ways. These calls do not extend to the market system, which socializes and institutionalizes selfish behavior. They do not extend to any government action, as the government is complicit in creating immorality and selfishness. They do not extend to all individuals either, as only those labeled as social drains, such as criminals, drug users, welfare recipients, and the poor, need change. Today's civic check infuses a substantive, worthwhile collective debate with pedagogy and vitriol. Its noise of recreating civic culture demeans cultural diversity and individual rights as it searches for a controlling *Zeitgeist* in the name of tradition and morality.

As mentioned, one of the principal complaints today is that an egoistic individualism pervades all social interaction. Tocqueville's double edge is most apparent here, as he describes the two variants of individualism that either complete or undermine democracy. While he thought America solved the potential ills of individualism wrongly understood with a continual, abiding interest in collective concerns, today a break exists between the individual and the public good. This break, and especially the apparent contradictions that emerge from individual behavior today, are the focus of today's civic health check. The changes in individual behavior from Tocqueville's time contribute to today's civic health debate. Thus, have profound changes occurred in how individuals view themselves and society since Tocqueville's age? Or, in Tocqueville's analysis how can he argue that America is a nation of joiners while simultaneously a country of individuals? Does a duality or tension exist in the American character—and thus expressed in our social action and political interaction—that produces mixed signals about our civic virtue and our democratic aspirations?

One common view today is that while once a powerful civic culture, backed by religious and moral traditions, informed American democracy, presently Tocqueville's individualism wrongly understood directs behavior. From this line of thought, rights have superceded the good. Individuals clamor to protect their immediate interests often at the expense of any public vision. Or, the workings of individualism have unintended but disastrous collective consequences. Today's civic debate, then, often calls for a return to the beneficial strength of the good aiding individual rights. This idea warrants action, but when not applied equally to all social, political, and economic processes, its meaning devolves into moral posturing with the brunt of the "new" obligations unduly heaved on those most lacking in all resources. In the end the poor, for instance, must deal with their economic condition as well as an inadequate, perhaps immoral, social stigma because of their station. In the simplest terms, why are American icons always wealthy?

In sum, it is essential to be cautious about how ideologues employ Tocqueville's observations. He does offer insight for today's civic discussion, but his biases and how his biases inform today's debate temper full-fledged support for his ideas. Before addressing some of his ideas, it is important to delve into the question of American individualism and how its present characteristics affect civic culture. Tocqueville's fear of individualism devolving into selfish egoism appears well-founded today. This produces a dichotomy between individual interests and the collective or public good. While this dichotomy fuels today's civic health check, I think it essential to explore a speculative topic that affects this dichotomy. This topic involves American individualism and how its expression seems contradictory at times. Is American society a bundle of inconsistencies, for instance, at once both politically astute and apathetic, at once both active and resigned, at once both interested and neglectful, and at once both involved and preoccupied, which make it difficult to decipher a general will and to offer meaningful public policies? Or, conversely, is American opinion less wanton and whimsical? Rather, it is resolute in some fundamental ideas, as Tocqueville would have us believe, but is prone to contradictory views given the changes in modern life during the twentieth century. For instance, citizens no longer express their political voice because of the obstacles created by bureaucracy and the growth of government's scale. These ideas and questions are elements of the civic virtue debate as they offer insight into the causes of behavior that foster the debate's superficial accusations of immorality. Thus, I want to ask a series of questions, or make several tentative observations about American individualism and its apparent dualities, that I know I cannot answer satisfactorily. I want to make initial stabs at answers with the idea that my attempts leave room for further discussion.

UNDERSTANDING APATHY

I ended the last chapter by stating a roiling social current exists. It seems that if America suffers from a lack of civic interaction, by definition then, individuals increasingly refrain from social and political activity. How, then, if individuals choose to not interact, does turmoil capture today's culture? Apathy and cynicism better describe this lack of interest and attention. Volumes have been written about the separation Americans feel toward their government and about their lack of influence in political issues in general. In fact, the term *politics* has a decidedly negative connotation in popular opinion today, where elected officials conduct "behind closed door" dealings with professional lobbyists for major corporate interests and then appease the public with evasive and meaningless jargon. Some argue that the public's cynicism is a type of defense mechanism against the world's complexity, from government's seeming distance from a person's life, as well as, ironically enough, government's overwhelming control in deciding how a person lives. In one sense, if people believe that public issues affect their lives yet they do not know how to affect these issues, then cynicism appears as a response to forces beyond their perceived control. In another sense, when people feel as if they cannot make choices about how to live because of governmental constraints, then cynicism results again from a perceived lack of control.

David Mathews does not delve into the psychology of cynicism that marks much of today's political attitudes, but he does describe some of its characteristics through Dewey's observations. He writes:

> Some time ago, John Dewey identified virtually all of the factors that lead to dysfunctional political cultures. People, he wrote, come to believe that they are "caught in the sweep of forces too vast to understand or master." Feeling overwhelmed by problems, people may turn inward, choosing not to participate in the decision-making process. When citizens find political issues too abstract and distant from their day-to-day existence and believe that the political system doesn't seem to value what they value, they may decide that the system will never pay attention to their concerns. . . . This is exactly the way some see the political arena. The point is that when politics is seen as separate from ordinary life, a separate realm and a specialized practice, the perception itself fuels a sense of powerlessness.[1]

Mathews' argument runs parallel to my inference in the previous chapter that the rights of equality demand greater citizen inclusion in the democratic process. What is important here is that political apathy and cynicism can result from mere perception and not actual noninvolvement. One does not need first-hand experience to feel powerless.

Appropriately, then, Mathews states that the one characteristic that underlies citizen action is the perception of change. It is not that change is assured, and it is not that citizens feel that through their efforts change necessarily will occur. Politics seems to come from the psychological state of possibility. Mathews states, "Participants in the Harwood discussions were clear and consistent about how a sense of possibility affected their involvement in civic projects. People said that they became active when they felt they might have some influence on events. . . . Just a sense that there was an opportunity to contribute seemed enough. People know that what they attempt may not always be successful and that the results of their efforts may not be what they had hoped."[2] What adversely affects people's perception of possibility is the structure of today's political process. Korten and Gordon unequivocally state that corporate interests pursue policies that destroy the middle-class family life associated with building the American Dream. Phillips, Sklar, and Wolff describe in harrowing detail the vast shifts in wealth as a result of corporate goals, with government complicity. Lasch, Kaus, and Walzer recognize the influence of class in American society and how the wealthy can choose to buy their way through the political process and buy their way out of society's most pressing problems. The political process itself minimizes the average person's voice in favor of professional lobbyists from the major economic, legal, and financial institutions. Against these perceptions—they in fact only need to be perceptions—citizen involvement in the democratic process seems far-fetched, a utopian vision.

Yet, against this bleak background, millions of citizens pursue political activity on a daily basis. Most of this activity has little to do with professionalized, corporate interests and the policy initiatives at the national level. It is politics located where Tocqueville recorded the uniqueness of American democracy. It is at the local, immediate level where people most intimately feel the effects of policy and political action. It is where associational life breeds civic virtue, and where people like my father toil to improve their corner of the country. Mathews notes that while cynicism runs rampant in society, there also exists a strong element of responsibility. In lieu of the moralizing that at times infuses today's civic debate, Americans display accountability for their political malaise. Against the powerful forces of corporate influence and government intractability, Mathews cites that, "People reason that reform has to begin with citizens themselves, that people have to be involved. . . . One person confessed, 'Generally speaking, the public is not very active in politics. It's like a snowball effect—you don't feel that you can have a voice; therefore, you don't participate, and you get farther and farther apart from your representative. . . . Maybe if more people were active, our representatives would be better.'"[3]

It seems in a political system that guarantees some basic human rights, the system guarantees little else. My argument is that if equality is one of these rights, even defined simply as the ongoing citizen involvement in the determination of public issues, then more action is necessary to guarantee this right. This action, though, comes from the freedom the state gives its citizens to pursue their lives and to make their government as they see fit. Citizens must choose to guarantee this right. Citizens have this responsibility to their government, to their society, and ultimately to themselves. The members of the government also have a responsibility, as elected representatives, to fight against narrowly defined interests, such as business or finance. Government must strike a balance between the collective good and narrowly-defined interests, and not subjugate the general will to any business agenda.

Moreover, American society simply does not socialize its future citizens toward any collective goal or interest. Religion and social tastes fashion a form of morality, which can be very powerful at times, but citizens are under no other collective requirement. No civil service exists, no volunteer work, no student education, nor any other sense of social obligation that demands the time and energy of American citizens. Private interests dominate socialization. While religion and community relationships still dictate some sense of duty and social behavior, other strong elements exist, like consumer marketing and educational demands, that preach private rewards over public interests. In this complex atmosphere, it is uncertain what citizens will do, for without an indelible example of the necessity of a commitment to their community or to their government, they act as mere economic units satisfying disparate and often imagined needs. Tocqueville aptly describes this social species as he writes, "Such folk owe no man anything and hardly expect anything from anybody. They form the habit of thinking of themselves in isolation and imagine that their whole destiny is in their own hands . . . and there is danger that [man] may be shut up in the solitude of his own heart."[4]

THE BASIS FOR AND TENSION OF INDIVIDUALISM

Cynical, isolated, and alone in their own hearts are common descriptions of Americans today. Most often, these descriptions decry the preeminence of the individual in society. Conservatives warn that important social norms and traditions are lost to the value granted by individual choices. Marxists point to the materialism of a consumer culture that undermines the ability of people to express their true freedom. Communitarians argue that the privileged position granted to individuals, as expressed in civil liberties, misses the importance of community values and commitments that help define the individual and those liberties. As opposed to the liberal view that individuals and their rights precede the good of the community, justice comprises not simply the community overriding individual preferences. Rather, justice becomes a complex mixture of individual rights in relation with, but not prior to, communal interests and requirements.[5] The good, then, exists as an interdependent force acting with and upon individual rights, and not as a counterweight, nor as a necessary opposing force upon individual choice.

The structure of the debate contributes to the enduring tension between the priority of individual rights and the values of the general good, or in today's terms rampant selfishness versus a respect for societal values and collective issues. In other words, if we cast today's civic virtue debate in terms of individual rights versus community obligations and respect, then we limit our understanding of the dynamic historical relationship between the two and the possible solutions that can emerge. As communitarian critiques note, a duality between the individual and the community, as liberalism commonly defines it, "has no room . . . for the idea that individuals might be or become constitutively attached to their community and thereby gain access to a type of human good that they could not achieve on their own."[6] This perspective differs markedly from the liberal tradition's emphasis on individual ability to secure goods independent of communal attachment. For communal attachment is often defined as a restraint on individual action, as a foe rather than as a developmental friend.

Thus, if so many criticize today's social and political interaction, or lack thereof, if citizens feel disconnected from government and isolated from each other socially, if these problems are pronounced enough to encourage a national debate about America's moral, political, and at times its socioeconomic conditions, then how have we come to this point? Has something gone wrong in our social and political makeup? Have institutions changed or not changed in response to social shifts? What was the original intent to ward off this duality between individual rights and common purposes? In fact, can we derive an original intent from America's founding, or was it a compromise of different interests that could never provide a satisfactory relationship between perhaps arbitrarily defined concepts?

Robert A. Goldwin explains that the founding fathers' understanding of the relationship between individual rights and the common good, while certainly not unanimous, did not emphasize the duality that we speak of today. Rather, they sought an institutional structure that wove together private and public interests so that acting for one was inextricably tied to securing the other. He writes:

The American solution to the age-conflict of private rights and public duties was not to speak of obligations, but to develop a certain character and behavior of citizens by designing a regime with institutions that encourage the pursuit of private advantage through public activity. The founders had in mind town councils, state legislatures, jury duty, voting for officials at local, state, and federal levels, lobbying, organizing of interest groups—all those activities that often make private-sector and public-sector activities almost indistinguishable and certainly inseparable. Experience in the exercise of political rights would habituate the self-seeking individual in behavior that was moderate, considerate of others, conciliatory, civil, and compromising, very much like that of a truly public-spirited citizen. A man who firmly believes that "honesty is the best policy" and is honest in his dealings for the sake of policy rather than for the sake of honesty will be, in his visible actions and habits, indistinguishable from the man who is honest for the sake of honesty.

The American constitutional scheme . . . does not seek to balance rights and duties, nor does it encourage talk about rights *versus* duties. Rights are too likely to win out in every such contest. Only rights have a sufficient natural power to counter rights successfully. The discourse of the founders is full of talk about the rights and interests of the people and of the community as a whole but nearly silent about duties.[7]

Goldwin's review of the founders' democratic theory stands in stark contrast to Tocqueville's observations of America fifty years into its democratic practice. While it seems that both claim it is necessary to secure democracy by intertwining private and public interests, Goldwin's analysis states that a concern for the public interest was not necessary to secure it. For Tocqueville, it was essential to America's democratic success that the individual recognize the importance of acting for the collective good. Moreover, while Tocqueville witnessed those civic activities that guaranteed democracy's well-being, Goldwin notes that although the founders sought to create a civic character, it was not essential for those moral habits of the heart to exist for democracy to flourish. Rather, the founders focused less on character and more on structural arrangements to secure democratic practice. It is obvious that Tocqueville's observations reveal behavior that was conducive to a well-ordered democracy. Tocqueville's accounts saw that democracy depended on the people's concern for the public good. However, this civic behavior was less of a fundamental component of democracy for the founders. Similar to their ideas concerning great statesmen, the founders thought that while civic virtue would advance democratic government, institutions must check private interests as virtue may not always be possible. For them, democracy could flourish even if people remained motivated by private interest. The system's success was in the design of the government; it was not dependent upon the citizenry's morality.

If Goldwin's interpretation is accurate, then today's cries for greater civic virtue reflects the founders' resistance to demand any kind of civic character as a linchpin for democratic government. In other words, today's civic advocates call for a moral character on which the founding fathers thought better not to depend. Instead, the Federalists advocated structural supports for the expression of civic virtue. In fact, the Federalists devised a structure that never needed truly civic behavior. Civic behavior would result from the intimate connections between the public expression of private actions. As Goldwin points out, apparently a person need not be publicly interested for the public interest to emerge. From this theoretical beginning it is apparent why America suffers from a civic virtue deficit today. If in fact virtue is missing from today's politics, it is first because virtue was never a cornerstone of American democracy. Again, if civic virtue exists, then it benefits democracy; but the founders never constructed a government based on the civic virtue of its citizens.

The founders, if listening to today's debate, would emphasize that today's lack of virtue proves that it cannot be a basis for government. But more importantly, if virtue cannot be depended upon, then today's calls for greater virtue miss other, perhaps more essential, elements of why democracy's health is failing. For as Madison warned, "But what is government itself but the greatest of all reflections on human nature? If men were angels, no government would be necessary. . . . This policy of supplying, by opposite and rival interests, the defect of better motives, might be traced through the whole system of human affairs, private as well as public."[8] Perhaps part of the reason why American politics and society lack strong civic virtue today is because the founders thought it foolish to rely on its presence at all times to sustain democracy. If government, then, bases itself on self-interest and not on civic virtue, most likely that behavior will be accepted and institutionalized. As a result, today's concern for civic virtue either misses the founders' original intent, or it recognizes the paucity of a government based wholly on self-interest. In short, we lack civic virtue today because civic virtue was never an instrumental element for democracy's functioning.

However, civic virtue, while not institutionalized in the government's structure, was for Tocqueville one of the important facets of America's democratic success. Goldwin states that nothing was or is asked of citizens in terms of duties, whereas rights are described in detail. However, while the founders never institutionalized duties as they did rights, they did depend on norms and customs to establish duties. One of Jefferson's worries was that over time Americans would lose sight of the reasons why these norms of self-government are important. As the battle for freedom ebbs and freedom is taken for granted, the duty to participate to guarantee its preservation fades. Also, in the Federalist's structure, self-interest seemed the only necessary consideration in pursuing the collective interest. Or is it? Today self-interest clouds the one fundamental agreed-upon tenent of democratic government: democracy demands, to which my definition of equality alludes, an ongoing civic interaction. The Federalist structure confuses this basic requirement of democracy.

My purpose in this historical review is to note the tension that the founding period established between rights and duties and between self-interests and the general good. The Federalists defined human nature as self-serving and designed government to accommodate and incorporate this tendency. Today's call for greater civic virtue does not look to the founding period for its inspiration, as the founding reveals a government based on self-interest. Rather, it is Tocqueville's observations about a vibrant civic culture infused by strong associations that guide today's search for a more meaningful politics. If we examine the political theory that underlies this country's government, we see clearly that its negative interpretation of human nature—and thus its dismissal of civic virtue to play an integral role in the government's operation—steers people toward selfishness. In short, if we believe people are selfish, and design a system that incorporates selfishness, then we assure and legitimate selfishness. Today's individualism can be understood as the product of this country's political system, obviously stoked by this country's economic system too. Any lamentations about America's loss of civic virtue must confront our thoroughly self-interested beginnings.

This insight heightens the moral tension between acting in self-interested ways and the equally prized virtues of community service and building a public perspective. It seems current society presents the individual with a confounding selection of choices. On one hand, economic assumptions and contemporary consumerism encourage the individual to pursue self-interests. This is the so-called benefit of capitalism as the market responds to consumer preferences. Also, the Federalist design argues that collective goods result from the pursuit of private interests.

In much of contemporary society, from the workplace to the grocery store to any civic encounter, this liberal conception of society teaches its citizens to act as selfish automatons. On the other hand, a host of moral assumptions underscore social relations that devalue selfish actions and nurture consideration for and pursuit of collectivist goals. Religion inculcates unselfish acts and the virtues of sharing, tolerance, and respect for others. Tocqueville, along with many other theorists, spoke to the role of tradition and customs that tie people together as communities, each with their unique sense of history and propriety. These bonds also teach individuals how to act, but not as self-interested consumers. Rather, these forces dictate commitments to others, to historical legacies, to interests and ideas that extend beyond the marketplace and the political system. As a consequence, every individual is an amalgamation of these two opposing forces, each providing a system of conduct in direct opposition to the other.

Today, many social conservatives emphasize the lost of civic virtue by noting the loss of morality and traditions, the consequence of social changes that need revision. At the same time, these conservatives overlook the power of both the market and political indoctrination to teach selfish pursuits. With the loss of tradition, the individual becomes ever more selfish in orientation—at least in theory. But if the forces of tradition and morality are rebuilt, perhaps through a religious revival such as the growth of the Religious Right and the Promise Keepers, this simply would reinvent the tension for each individual between the opposing forces of selfishness and civility. In sum, it seems obvious today that the market and political teachings have overcome social concerns and moral sensibilities. To solve this dilemma, we need to pay greater attention to the market and political system, rather than fix our attention exclusively or extensively to the social and moral condition of society. As the civic virtue debate digresses from these areas, people confront the difficulty in reconciling how they must act in the economic, political, and social realms. The customary behavior in these arenas diverges greatly from the behavior most often learned and expected in the familial or private realm.

CONTEMPORARY CHALLENGES TO CIVIC LIFE

In addition to evidence that associational life was nurtured by the federal government and biased in favor of the wealthy during Tocqueville's age, important changes since the early nineteenth century make any return to America's civic golden age a foolish pursuit. Most importantly, Max Weber writes about the debilitating effects of bureaucratization on individual freedom. The rational ordering of society—intimately tied to increasing the efficiency and productivity of the capitalist system—undermines the spirit of creativity and initiative that infuses human life. But rationality is a process that has numerous advantages, so that individuals are caught between the goods from rationality and the goods from their humanity. As Gerth and Mills write, "For Weber, capitalism is the embodiment of rational impersonality; the quest for freedom is identified with irrational sentiment and privacy. Freedom is at best a tarrying for loving companionship and for the cathartic experience of art as a this-worldly escape from institutional routines."[9] In this view, both modern capitalism and its bureaucratic handmaiden function to rob individuals of their essential character. Similar to what Tocqueville relates about the workman losing his creativity as he specializes in one task, Weber worries over the social and political consequences of the primacy given the economic process. He states, "The question is: how are democracy and freedom in the long run at all possible under the domination of highly developed capitalism? Freedom and democracy are only possible where the resolute will of a nation not to allow itself to be ruled like sheep is permanently alive. We are 'individualists' and partisans of 'democratic' institutions 'against the stream' of material constellations."[10] Once again, individuals face a tension between everyday areas in their lives. To assume that an intelligent person knows how to behave given the arena—self-interested in economic and political affairs, community-oriented in local concerns and personal matters—misses the idea that different realms need not demand different behavior. A rationally-ordered society with a capitalist economy may be best run with a democratic disposition.

For my purposes, Tocqueville's and Weber's worries center on not just the dehumanizing functions of the capitalist and bureaucratic process but also on the difficulties individuals confront on a daily basis to counter or to challenge these embedded and privileged processes. To explain, Weber differentiates between two forms of rationality. The individual uses one form to understand and assess the essential and profound meanings of life—a rationality that deciphers what is meaningful for each person. The other form of rationality is one of an instrumental kind. It evaluates, processes, and finds the most efficient routes to satisfy goals and objectives. Weber worried that instrumental reasoning was becoming preeminent, and thus people were replacing efficiency for meaning and fulfillment. Thus, Weber thought when the rationality of science, the market, or any bureaucratic enterprise replaced the value of what he labeled the substantive search for meaning, people ineluctably became separated from the objects and choices that make them happy. Over time, this separation produces what he called the "disenchantment of the world," as instrumental rationality obscures the search for happiness.[11]

From Weber's ideas, today's individual finds meaning in a rationality that has little public expression and even less public value. But this is not a simple problem of "everyone-else-is-doing-it," so I should do similarly. As Tocqueville notes, while popular opinion is a sinister and subtle form of modern tyranny, people can and often do challenge it. Instead, the problem of instrumental rationality is that while it destroys what Weber thought was essential to being human, it simultaneously provides apparent benefits—a sense of equality, efficiency, stability — in how humans function and interact. To this end, the answers of scaling back government and creating stronger moral codes to solve America's current civic crisis address some of the symptoms but not nearly enough of the causes of civic decline. Impersonal bureaucracy may still exist at the local level, and the idea of bureaucracy—with its attempt at treating all people equally—appeals to the democratic spirit. But it is also true that the problems that foster civic decline, such as the vast discrepancy between the rich and poor, also discourage bureaucratic equality as people pay their way through any governmental inquiry, review, or process.

Weber notes the example of workers resisting the changes in the twentieth century to civil service reform. On the one hand, civil service protects the worker from arbitrary and ruthless bosses, providing for equality through a definitive accounting of promotion, pay, and overall treatment. On the other hand, civil service undercuts the power of local leaders to accrue powers of appointment and confer those positions to favored individuals. Bosses no longer have power; power resides in *the process*. Although this may create more equal conditions over time, and thus it is preferable and inevitable in an ever-larger system of economic and political production, individuals resist these changes as accountability is often lost. Weber's example of civil service resistance is instructive in that it reveals the tensions inherent in modern life. People recoil against change that benefits them. While face-to-face interaction is necessary and essential in some social relations, increasingly more modern situations demand increasingly less physical interaction. In a sense people must give their personal trust over to others and to situations of which they have little knowledge and control. What results is an increasing unease with and isolation from the forces that guide a person's life. People may increasingly see themselves as unable to guide their own lives. Bureaucracy estranges people from their ability to choose their own ends. Or, because they now must place trust in systems and people beyond their choosing, people grow detached from what they can and cannot control. If either detached or estranged, it seems accurate to claim that cynicism is a reluctant response to cope with modern life. Unfortunately, detachment or estrangement are exactly the behaviors that Weber would argue cannot sustain democracy or freedom against the powers of high-technology, globalizing capitalism and its political compatriots.

As opposed to the insidious working of an ever-increasing bureaucratic world and the covert pressure to compete in an ever-competitive capitalist economy, DeLue also notes personal constraints to the possibilities of a civil society. He notes that:

Individuals must themselves assume responsibility for their lives by recognizing that often enough the barriers that obstruct the realization of their highest hopes are not external ones at all, but internal ones. . . . [P]eople, who understand the nature of the aspirations arising from the higher faculties of the mind, may be unable to pursue these aspirations. The tragedy in this circumstance is that people lack an ability to achieve what they know is best for themselves, and the central reason for this condition is a failure of their own will. . . . Here, the iron cage is not something we are placed into, but it is something that we allow to occur within our own lives. . . . A civil society will survive only as long as its people have the vitality to confront with courage and with the fortitude of a strong will the challenges of their particular lives and to make of their lives what they know from honest reflection, in the Foucault manner, is best for them.[12]

DeLue enunciates a popular theme today that demands individual responsibility for one's choices. Obviously, for people to maintain a strong civil society, they must be accountable for nurturing this environment through their actions. At the personal level, each must be aware of what is best for both themselves and others. This, then, is a problem that DeLue does not address, for to achieve what is best for oneself, perhaps in true Nietzchean artistic expression, may conflict with the aims of civil society. This dilemma is the source of today's civic debate, as many believe Americans trumpet individual goals at the expense of social conditions and public interests.

More importantly, I emphasize the conflicting options individuals confront on a daily basis, and the socialization toward certain choices allows them to seem both natural and predetermined. In this sense, DeLue's passage presents notable understanding. However, after describing the economic and political obstacles that guarantee the diminution of individual choice, or even the difficulty in knowing what to choose and how one's choices affect others, DeLue's insight does not account for these barriers. If the modern economic and political systems present significant barriers for individual choice, then are individuals responsible for actions and ideas that are beyond their control? What better example of modern cynicism and the difficulty of expressing one's best ideas in true Foucault fashion than the collective problems of unhealthy air and water, mass transit deficiencies, and any other wasteful practice that contributes to America's over-consumption and pollution of the world. Is it true that one person's choice not to drive an automobile will change the brown clouds that hover over Los Angeles, Denver, Chicago, and New York?

To emphasize individual responsibility, if only as one element of other detrimental processes like economic change, as the source of social problems thoroughly undervalues the profound effects economic and social changes have on individual behavior. More pointedly, when you create an economically and politically just environment, then one can argue forcefully for personal accountability. As it is today, individuals must still be responsible for their actions in an unjust and contradictory world. Ironically, the civic virtue that does exist comes from individuals acting against the forces and processes that make up present society. Our civic virtue, then, perhaps does not extend to our collective problems because each of us musters all available energy to fight daily against the inexorable enemies of economic control and political arbitrariness. Furthermore, DeLue's definition of obsession runs a slippery slope between socially destructive individual behavior and the kind of mindset and behavior necessary for the individual expression of true freedom. Who determines when my actions become obsessions? Is Tocqueville's oppressive public opinion the judge? DeLue ascribes some underlying rational criteria, expectedly monitored by our own judgments, of which any Foucault reading presents as a socially-contrived system of the powerful and the powerless. If we are the judges of our actions, and there is little external social pressure, then this definition misses the acculturation that informs both Tocqueville's and Foucault's work. If, though, strong socializing forces control what we come to choose as our expression of freedom, is it certain that we have come to know intelligently and personally what it is that allows us to be challenged, invigorated, and excellent? We may know what society wants us to be and do, but is that true individual freedom? Again, the individual faces considerable and critical tension. DeLue's passage presents the tensions I argue make uncertain any definitive and sustainable course of decision-making and action in today's world.

NATURE AND NURTURE IN THE HUMAN ELEMENT

Thus far, I argue that within the swirl of complexity that comprises modern society, rife with uncertain consequences from economic behavior, political self-interest, and bereft of any lasting idea of the public good, individuals encounter numerous tensions that confound well-meaning intentions and obscure clear courses of social action. Yet, I shy away from the idea, which is often echoed today, that these tensions are the innate structuring of people. Does human nature explain the gulf between expectations and reality, between individual desires and individual action? It seems reasonable that our political apathy and inattention explain our political problems. But to secure blame for America's civic decline on a lack of citizen responsibility belittles the power Weber recognizes in the inevitable growth of bureaucratic organizations in modern society, belittles the power Tocqueville and Foucault recognize in popular opinion dictating social conformity, and belittles the power nearly all social scientists recognize in the capitalist economy to influence, if not control, all facets of political and social life. Certainly, we are more than mere passive subjects victimized by an endlessly cruel economic system—a view often attributed to Marxist critiques of capitalism.

I hesitate, though, to describe Americans as wholly active agents capable of recognizing the subtleties of power that affect their lives and greatly influence their choices. For although individuals in theory retain the freedom to choose lifestyles, they are also socialized to act in their self-interest in the marketplace, yet to act with public-spirited self-interest in political matters, and yet again to act with selfless compassion and tolerance in their personal affairs. If different arenas call for different behavior and different understanding of others, then it is no doubt an open question as to why society at times demands selflessness and at other times demands selfishness. Individuals simply conform to these norms of behavior, but confront these tensions daily with a host of responses. Some ignore addressing these tensions. Some become cynical while others cannot find solace even in contemptuous thinking. Many others, I venture, find peace with this duality by focusing their energies on personal issues, and while noticing public concerns, spend little time engaged in issues beyond their immediate worlds.

Our lack of civic virtue may simply reveal the primacy we grant self-interested attitudes in our economic and political thinking. Most Americans may not agree with a self-interested basis for public and governmental action, but as the founders thought, this cautious approach ensures the worst will not occur. The downside to this approach is that it may also ensure the best will not occur. At the individual level, in the Tocquevillean sense, the emotional wound inflicted by acting against the social norm in the economic or political arena is not worth the benefit of—of what?—resolving this selfish-selfless, private-public tension. Social and familial relations cannot compete with the predominance of self-interest, especially with the power of the marketplace to invade social thinking. We are left, then, with our disenchantment with the world. It is these powers of socialization and social structure that give America its present civic crisis, and not some innate human wiring that casts each into an empty quandary over unrealized expectations.

Given this view, let me restate an earlier tension that lends credence to the power of human nature to create social and personal dilemmas. We are very much Aristotle's social beings, and we give great meaning to how others view us. Again, this is Tocqueville's exemplary insight into human nature: that popular opinion has the power in times of democratic equality to stifle differences and to exert a mental force to conform peoples' behavior. To have oneself and one's ideas validated by public opinion satisfies the human urge to be accepted and be "part of a group." In negative terms, Tocqueville states the disastrous possibilities for democracy and freedom if citizens act as each others' reciprocal lemmings. However, the tension Tocqueville notes is that in times of equality people also exhibit actions and tastes to differentiate themselves from their neighbors. In America, this differentiation primarily exists in economic wealth, as the privileges of aristocracy and hierarchical status are nonexistent. If Tocqueville is accurate, it is possible to extrapolate that the energy invested to differentiate economically takes away from the energy necessary to partake politically. In turn, as citizens focus energy away from the political process, it becomes the domain of entrenched and professionalized interests.

However, what Tocqueville misses is that when people act to differentiate themselves, they have agreed to some prior assumptions about their abilities to differentiate. They have agreed that to express their freedom in the economic realm relies on the agreement of some measure of rough equality, typically an equality of opportunity to pursue their economic freedom. This is, or perhaps was, the American Dream; through their efforts everyone can achieve a decent, comfortable life. Here, the ideas of freedom through effort and initiative link strongly with the equality of opportunity for all to gain. Interestingly, what we gain by economically differentiating ourselves in times of equality—for example a sense of identity and success—we in turn lose by disregarding the political freedoms that foster the value of equality in the first place. We lose our political freedoms if we focus solely on our economic freedoms. Thus, the duality that Tocqueville establishes between liberty and equality is artificial, as equality is the expression of political freedom, and true individual liberty evolves from a measure of social and political equality. In short, to differentiate oneself from others, in a sense to express one's liberty, depends on a well-defined notion of equality that allows individuals to pursue their freedoms.

But Tocqueville understands this, as his ideas about individualism properly and wrongly understood show. He knew that individualism, through its expression of individual liberty, was a beneficial attribute for all people. He also knew that if individualism was not tempered with the personal characteristics and social conditions of moderation, discipline, respect for tradition, customs, and individual and collective virtues, then individualism would devolve into rampant selfishness. To benefit society, individualism needs a significant degree of control. The question is where does this control of individualism begin and continue? Today's civic virtue debate focuses blame squarely on the shoulders of individuals, and principally those individuals who are marginalized in or by society. Here, the disintegration of the family, the loss of religion and social stability, the increase in crime and drug use, and the lax moral attitudes are all signs of individual digressions. An alternative view is that while individuals must take responsibility for their actions, society must be held accountable also for the behavior it promotes. Strong families still must confront the power of advertising and economic selfishness. As Gordon explains, teen pregnancy, drug use, and crime are indications of a lack of equal economic conditions and of governmental economic policy in general. Culture wars are easy to cite and dismiss as inexorable social trends. Class wars place problems at the feet of every democratic citizen.

In less abstract words, to believe that it is human nature to differentiate oneself from others undervalues the social contract of society that allows individuals to express their choices. To emphasize one without the effect of the other provides a simplistic and often inaccurate account of their interaction. When right replaced might as the basis of human interaction, then the power of society to influence human behavior became intimately bound to any notion of human agency. Consequently, how does my view of the inextricably tied active agent or passive subject human confront the tensions inherent in modern life? Cynicism, apathy, and withdrawal are common political or public responses. But at the personal level, people often find meaning through their families and religion. As for families, today's civic debate emphasizes the deleterious effects of a pronounced divorce culture. The traditional family provides for an environment that fosters the ideal civic virtue, as this thinking goes. But today more questions than answers emerge from such a statement. James Morone argues:

According to the 1990 census, more than 79 percent of the households include a married couple, down undramatically from 82.5 percent a decade earlier. . . . Of course, not all marriages work and not all families are good for children. . . . What is a proper family? What is the social institution that we are trying to revive? . . . We have lost our consensus about the nature of the family—or, more precisely, about the nature of the woman's role. . . . This does not mean giving up. . . . But remember that the forces moralizing for marital commitment strongly disagree about what a good marriage is. And the golden era they recall was structured on an inequity that is, happily, fading.[13]

The idea here is not to repeat my earlier argument about the economic impediments to a life after divorce, or to describe the effects of the social stigmas attached to it, or still to note the simplistic attitudes and remedies to changing social conditions. I seek only to emphasize the difficulty of the issue for the individual citizen to reconcile—with a knowledge of research and changing social customs—in some intelligent fashion. No woman need stay with a cheating husband, but many did and still do. No woman need depend on her husband's wage to care for her, but many did. Just as the nature of civic virtue may occur today in different areas than the traditional ones to which we are accustomed, changing American society calls for a more thorough examination of what constitutes all social relations. A traditional family did not treat women as equals, and is that what we hope to return to when we seek a vibrant civic society?

If the idea of the family is difficult to define today, the idea of religion as a moralizing or simply personally meaningful force also raises difficult questions. First, Morone cites statistics that reveal America's lasting religious tone. He states, "According to the Gallup Organization, 95 percent of Americans profess a faith in God—a number that has scarcely budged in years. . . . More than three-quarters of the population belong to a church, a steady 40 percent say they went this week, and 9 percent claim to go to church 'several times a week.' Only the last figure, reported by the National Opinion Research Center, has changed much in the past two decades—and it is up 30 percent."[14] However, these statistics mislead if the conclusion is that America's religiosity has remained both strong and stable. For America's religious attitudes have undergone change in the last thirty years. Barry Kosmin and Seymour Lachman explain:

One of the most important features of the religious outlook of baby boomers is "religious privatization," a concept that explains the cultural shift to individualism within this generation. It encourages personal needs and interests in the shaping of religious commitment and ideology. As a result, religious insight is increasingly based on personal experience, and the church becomes a means to meeting personal objectives. When faith is a personal affair, ties to institutional religion are reduced.

Another important key to understanding baby boomers, and modern Americans as a whole, is to gain insight into their adoption of "cultural egalitarianism" as a creed. They increasingly question all authority, hierarchy, and domination. They show less loyalty to denomination and congregation, and are less likely to acknowledge the church as the source of religious insight or its authority on matters of religious truth and doctrine. It is as if they have collectively imbibed George Bernard Shaw's statement that "every profession is a conspiracy against the laity." . . . The clergy have responded by dispensing as far as possible with their clerical collars and other robes of office, opening up their ranks to women, and adapting their once-powerful role as pastors into that of enablers, facilitators, and managers of communities of the faithful.[15]

Increasingly individualistic religious attitudes, as with society in general, significantly alter religion's role in a person's life. Americans are still religious but less deferential and accepting as they once were. Religion appears less as the definitive source and more as an additional source of meaning and direction in American life.

Are, then, the consequences of religion's privatization as severe as undermining moral standards and eroding communities? Given the robust number of Americans who maintain religious attitudes and attend services, it seems that the individualizing trends promote a healthy questioning of religious ideas and meanings. They encourage thought and reflection about how to nurture children and the approach different religious ideas afford human interaction. This questioning and the "shopping" for a specific religious brand seems appalling given traditional approaches. But this shopping informs and engages. It generates commitment and appeal. It promotes interest and lasting bonds. It promotes the same kind of process necessary for obtaining political information and knowledge. Making an intelligent decision after informed discussion through exhaustive research seems more apt and conducive to supplying life-long meaning, but many deride it as simply untraditional. If tradition is simply signing on to where one's parents signed on, be it a religion or a political party, then tradition seems as much a thoughtless controlling mechanism as it is a conduit for moral and civic interest. In the end, civic attention comes from interest, and commitment—the very characteristics today's religious shopping describes.

The difficulty here lies in the difference between active agent and passive subject. If today's civic remedies seek a return to traditional methods, either in the family or in religious attitudes, then they seek only a passive subject who adheres to social control mechanisms. This may be an overly dramatic rendition of the past, but today's critics of our civic culture often revere the past in overly simplified ways. Moreover, and to heart of my argument, religion's privatization places enormous emphasis on individuals. It forces them to become informed and make coherent choices about personal attitudes and social concerns. While I just stated this provides the foundation for an engaged citizenry, it also presents a host of issues that often confuse people. Issues no longer have easy, simple solutions. Their complexity and the viability of arguments to both sides of a debate create several options. Often, people fall back on quick answers, with knee-jerk reaction and little thought. Other times, research shows people view issues and events through an established lens, so that no matter the ideas or information presented, an individual's need for ideological or attitudinal structure mutes any open, thoughtful exploration. My point is that social change demands patience and great reserves of time to examine and contemplate the effects and possibilities. Most of us do not grant ourselves the time to undertake these examinations in either the larger, more distant social realm or in our personal ideas and attitudes. As a case in point, much like political party affiliation, religious denominations are rarely chosen based on informed research and belief systems. Instead, one's parents most often determine one's party and church, and from this socialization people create their belief systems. Thus, people come to their beliefs and views after making a decision on how and where to express them rather than expressing them after they decide what their beliefs and views are. This process exudes a convenience-stop mentality. In the end, these social changes add informational complexity to American life, and this complexity further confounds a citizen's search for understanding and meaning.

FROM ATOMS TO CHAOS

The government's structure and its original intent precludes more than fosters a common vision. Modern organizational changes distance people from each other and from politics in general. Standard operating procedures trumpet impartiality and equality at the cost of deliberative give-and-take and conciliation. Despite the fairness that it promotes, what turns many off to bureaucracy is its ruthless efficiency and its lack of human concern. Rules and regulations demand little discretion, and thus less and less sensitivity, perception, knowledge, and awareness. The human element disappears, and in turn people act less as friends, colleagues, neighbors, and sentient beings. Even traditional mechanisms of meaning, such as family and religion, have undergone or are undergoing dramatic social changes that present challenges for private and public behavior.

Often, the issue of trust is at the heart of the debate over society's apparent loss of civic virtue. Modern life is no longer lived at the corner grocery and over neighborhood fences. Now, as the scope and scale of life expand, people's work and interests spread their lives over greater distances and in many directions. Most people express little trust in the federal government, but this distrust seems natural given the distance between the citizen and government today and the proximity necessary for trust to occur. Once again, people encounter social changes that demand their time and energy to maintain interpersonal relations and public concerns. Besides government, today's communication technology, like television before it, comes with the pronouncements of its potential to unite and bond citizens throughout the country and the world. After some initial experimentation, it is certain that while it connects some, it also allows others to disengage, especially from any public dialogue. Civil society, then, is not nurtured wholly by government or by technology, but by citizens who trust one another. Adam Seligman notes, however that, "Here we see . . . the paradox of modern society, rooted in abstract and generalized trust, which in the political sphere is represented by the universalization of citizenship. . . . The very universalization of trust in citizenship, however, undermines that concrete mutuality and shared components of the moral community upon which trust is based. Hence the call for a return to civil society."[16] The dilemma is that what appears as a beneficial building-block for all social relations demands a limited, particularistic conception and use.

Is America's concern over civic virtue simply its disillusionment or disappointment with the scale of society and government? If the power of trust is lost when we apply it to broad levels of interaction, then are the calls for reducing government's size while enhancing moral, religious, and civic traditions the obvious answers for curing American ills? In some quarters, these are the necessary remedies. However, while government's size can be controlled—or we would like to think so—it seems dubious to think that society can be downsized. More accurately, it is improbable that Americans will restrict the market economy's scale so that Wal-Marts, Home Depots, and Gap stores will become wholly local enterprises. Ithaca, New York, experiments with local money, which is used to support businesses and services only in the city,[17] and Jane Jacobs' idea of import substitution favors building regional economies throughout the country instead of one national or global economy.[18]

If these economic changes seem unlikely, and thus our civic life seems questionable, it is due to a more fundamental American outlook that comprises all facets of our life and how we view ourselves. It is not just our individualism, in that we see ourselves and others as distinct and separate from each other, but our attitudes about how we interact and what—if anything other than a social contract based on fear or self-interest—binds us together. While communitarianism is a relatively recent political philosophy that challenges the primacy of the individual and prefers to view each person as embedded in a lineage of tradition and social relations that alter how that individual functions socially and politically, I want to point out a similar questioning approach to the typical understanding of the isolated, rational individual. This approach applies the ideas of scientific theory to political phenomena, and it begins with the reappraisal of the individual's wholly distinct separateness. William Bennett Munro begins this examination as he states:

> The American philosophy of government has exalted the individual citizen beyond all reason. It treats him as the incarnation of the Unknown Soldier. . . . Hence it is the national habit to think of social control and individual freedom in terms of hostility to each other, whereas it is only through the one that the other can be realized under the conditions of today. For even as every molecule of physical matter is conditioned and directed by those with which it interacts, so the individual citizen is similarly motivated and controlled by the influence of those with whom he associates.[19]

This is hardly novel, and some would see it as a move to give politics and human relations greater scientific cogency with the hope of locating controllable variables with which to isolate the most beneficial means and accomplish the most desired ends. This is not my agenda. I want to point out, as others have with different methods, that a specific conception of the individual limits the options that are available. As Benjamin Barber explained earlier in *Strong Democracy*, Christa Daryl Slaton highlights the preferences accorded the individual in political thinking. She lists, in line with this scientific perspective, that atomism, indivisibility, commensurability, and mutual exclusivity are the general characteristics that we apply to citizens.[20] She, among others, understands the consequences of these fundamental attributes as a society beholden to liberal democracy, where each is left to pursue rationally determined wants in fair competition with each other for private property. In essence, this understanding of people fuels the difficulties people confront to attain or to exist in this worldview.

Moreover, I want to note that while quantum theory gave insight into the inadequacies of a Newtonian conception of the world, today chaos and complexity theories add greater subtlety to any scientific—and in relation to any political and social—understanding. For the basic approach of these recent ideas is to acknowledge the profound effects of rather simple actions or causes. The most overused analogy here is that the motion of the butterfly's wings in some distant region of the globe can ultimately influence the power and scope of a hurricane in some other location. In a sense, we are all interconnected, and within this notion of innumerable effects, some notion of order can be dissected. How does this apply to citizens, politics, and civic virtue? M. Mitchell Waldrop explains with this story:

> "Every democratic society has to solve a certain problem," says [William Brian] Arthur. "If you let people do their own thing, how do you assure the common good?" . . . [I]n the United States, the ideal is maximum individual freedom—or as Arthur puts it, "letting everybody be their own John Wayne and run around with guns." However much that ideal is compromised in practice, it still holds mythic power. . . . But increasing returns cut to the heart of that myth. If small events can lock you in to any of several possible outcomes, then the outcome that's actually selected may *not* be the best. And that means that maximum individual freedom— and the free market—might *not* produce the best of all possible worlds.[21]

Increasing returns describes a process whereby positive feedback develops for a product, service, or belief so that others begin to favor its existence and accept it as customary. Waldrop gives several examples of increasing returns: the preference of gasoline over steam engines for automobiles, the preference to develop nuclear power over other sources, and the preference of VHS to Beta tapes. The heart of employing these scientific analogies is simply that American society may be the result of some unexpected and wholly unpredicted results that are antithetical to our ideals and undermine our original intentions. In fact, this is the insight of any collective action problem, where rational individual behavior produces unintended and sometimes disastrous collective results. But more importantly, these examples show again the complexity and inherent difficulties that the individual must navigate to make meaning of life. Perhaps despite our best efforts to nurture a vibrant civic life, our efforts may undermine our very goals due to unexpected effects. Or, our efforts may run into obstacles created by our other goals, or others' goals, so that any consistent actions to attack social and political problems can be frustrated by initial attitudes and actions.

An inexact example of this may be Jonathan Rauch's analysis of what he calls "demosclerosis." He explains that this is a disease that prohibits collective action, and its cause comes from the recent methods society uses to express its interests. By creating an interest group to lobby Congress for nearly every interest in society, lobbying groups have increased exponentially in the last twenty to thirty years. In turn, though, the multitude of lobbies have increased the pressure on representatives to respond to the variety of groups, not wanting to turn away potential voters. Moreover, the astronomical number of lobbies now simply increases the legislative and representative workload and inundates Congress with an abundance of particularized interests. Thus, while an individual group's intent was simple access and representation, the collective result, Rauch argues, is backlog and political stalemate.[22]

In keeping with the chapter's theme, then, in addition to the growing complexity of the world in which the individual must learn to cope with new modes of social interaction, the citizen also faces the difficult task of understanding a society in which good intentions can produce uncertain outcomes. A system that treats everyone equally also alienates some when it prohibits human understanding. The political system requests ongoing participation as it produces aberrant decisions. At the personal level, social behavior and attitudes change as society changes, and society readjusts to individual actions. The positive feedback loop endlessly reinvents the challenge for each person, and thus meaning for the individual in civic interaction and personal behavior remains elusive. In any collective endeavor, such as civic activity and political participation, it is this elusive aspect of complexity that individuals confront daily. Little wonder that civic life may not measure up to some idealized standard. Little wonder that constant calls for a more vital politics exist. Little wonder that changing social institutions and changing social relations cast our focus internally and not to civic engagement. At last, then, little wonder our "disenchantment with the world" lingers.

NOTES

1. David Mathews, *Politics for the People: Finding a Responsible Public Voice* (Urbana, Ill.: University of Illinois Press, 1994), 34–35.

2. Ibid., 37.

3. Ibid., 39.

4. Alexis de Tocqueville, *Democracy in America*, ed. J. P. Mayer (New York: HarperPerennial, 1969), 508.

5. See Michael J. Sandel, *Democracy's Discontent: America in Search of a Public Philosophy* (Cambridge, Mass.: The Belknap Press of Harvard University Press, 1996), chapter 7. Also, see Stephen Mulhall and Adam Swift, *Liberals and Communitarians* (Cambridge, Mass.: Blackwell Publishers, 1992), chapter 3.

6. Stephen Mulhall and Adam Swift, *Liberals and Communitarians* (Cambridge, Mass.: Blackwell Publishers, 1992), 41.

7. Robert A. Goldwin, "Rights Versus Duties: No Contest," in *Ethics in Hard Times*, eds. Arthur L. Caplan and Daniel Callahan (New York: Plenum Press, 1981), 128–129.

8. James Madison, Federalist Paper No. 51, in *The Federalist Papers*, ed. Clinton Rossiter (New York: Penguin Books, 1961), 322.

9. H. H. Gerth and C. Wright Mills, *From Max Weber: Essays in Sociology* (New York: Oxford University Press, 1946), 73.

10. Ibid., 71.

11. Steven M. DeLue, *Political Thinking, Political Theory, and Civil Society* (Boston, Mass.: Allyn and Bacon, 1997), 280.

12. Ibid., 354.

13. James A. Morone, "The Corrosive Politics of Virtue," *The American Prospect*, no. 26 (May–June 1996): 37–38.

14. Ibid., 31-32.

15. Barry A. Kosmin and Seymour P. Lachman, *One Nation Under God: Religion in Contemporary American Society* (New York: Harmony Books, 1993), 233.

16. Adam B. Seligman, *The Idea of Civil Society* (New York: The Free Press, 1992), 187.

17. Ben Dobbin, "Local Money Works at Home," *Associated Press News*, reprinted in *The Syracuse Post-Standard* (July 1, 1996): Business section, B1-2.

18. Jane Jacobs' idea of import substitution discussed in Daniel Kemmis, *Community and the Politics of Place* (Norman, Okla.: University of Oklahoma Press, 1990), 86–89.

19. William Bennett Munro, "Physics and Politics—An Old Analogy Revised," in *Quantum Politics: Applying Quantum Theory to Political Phenomena*, ed. Theodore L. Becker (Westport, Conn.: Praeger Publishers, 1991), 5–6.

20. Christa Daryl Slaton, "Quantum Theory and Political Theory," in *Quantum Politics*, 45–46.

21. M. Mitchell Waldrop, *Complexity: The Emerging Science at the Edge of Order and Chaos* (New York: Touchstone Book, 1992), 48.

22. Jonathan Rauch, *Demosclerosis: The Silent Killer of American Government* (New York: Times Books, 1994), chapter 3, 6.

5

∽

At the Confluence of Theory and Practice

When constitutions of granite can't save the planet what's to become
of us[1]
　　　　　　　　　　　　　　　　　　　　　　—The Tragically Hip

Every constitution then, and every law, naturally expires at the end of
19 years. If it be enforced longer, it is an act of force, and not of right.[2]
　　　　　　　　　　　　　　　　　　　　　　—Thomas Jefferson

Oiled today is America's latest squeaky wheel. Without an obvious national unifying foe, this typically conservative-led rant rails against
America's loss of individual and civic virtue. Displayed by the dubious
symptoms of welfare dependency, teen pregnancy, high crime rates, and
drug use, the overheated lament is that degeneracy infuses our culture. In
turn, news reporting seeks—if not creates—supposed emerging social
trends. Thus, we hear the squeaky reiterations about America's loss of
virtue, our loss of trust and security, our growing individualism, and the
deadening effects these all have on our public issues. Playing off the
American characteristic of cautious interest, this public hand-wringing
makes good copy, and thus its misleading information seeps into the collective consciousness. However, the evidence from how Americans act
counters this supposed social malaise. Galston and Levine report that,
"Judged against other industrialized nations, American civil society remains comparatively strong. . . . 82 percent of Americans belong to at least
one voluntary association. . . . Furthermore, Americans belong to (and
volunteer for) almost all types of groups at above-average rates."[3]

My message thus far seeks cautious analysis of today's civic virtue debate. Today's discussion focuses on the symptoms and not on the more fundamental social causes of our collective ills. A closer look reveals the basic discrepancies between a democratic government and a civic society wrapped in a capitalist economy. A society that favors the delicate balance between equality and liberty does not always find satisfying or meaningful outcomes solely from economic thinking. But corporate behavior and government complicity are only part of this puzzle's answer. The individual faces bewildering changes that surely make Jefferson's statement more relevant today than in his own time. Change replaces change so that traditions deal more with kishy relics from twenty years past, and not with the present institutions of family, church, and community. These institutions continue to exist, but social changes force them to alter their basic functions and roles.

Broad and significant obstacles exist to citizen politics. Our civic debate is born of good intentions, but its focus avoids the ineluctable forces that affect human nature and our social compact. The friction that truly demands oil comes not from the expression of our social and economic behavior. Rather, this friction originates from the larger issues of our social compact: of how we want to live together and of the relationships we seek from each other. As Jefferson prefers, the friction points to the element that I note comprises all democratic definitions. The citizens must continually involve themselves in their democracy. If we define ourselves as democratic and base our society on this agreement, then government action must encourage rather than restrain citizen action and input. Unfortunately, big government imposes on citizen activity, and corporate America also discourages individual initiative with its leviathan presence. Thus, given the economic and political obstacles that create their own traditions of bias and privilege, economics and politics afford citizens fewer and fewer opportunities to participate in America's democratic practice.

Interestingly, though, it is the irony inherent in the rock 'n roll lyric that provides democratic promise. For while it may be true that Americans' education allows them to confuse the Constitution with the Declaration of Independence, it is also true that for Americans a piece of granite does not make for democracy. While Americans revere their historical documents and their fundamental agreements, we also recognize that democracy succeeds not just from a piece of parchment. Democracy succeeds only in practice; only through action. Significant obstacles exist for a vibrant democratic politics and a robust citizen involvement, but despite these obstacles, millions of Americans today devote themselves to public issues on a daily basis. Neighbors create and join community watches, parents attend school functions and kids' soccer games, and local businesspeople group together to ward off the advances of America's largest corporations. Thus, the lyric captures Jefferson's hope. Despite our chagrin for today's social conditions, with its preference for Tocqueville's individualism wrongly understood and with its bias in favor of money, America exhibits a strong democratic tradition of interest and action. Yet, we must recognize that times have changed. Today's interest and action are not those of a generation ago. Politics has been manipulated by money's power and television's influence to devalue the process of civic action. In response, to find a vibrant politics demands insight into where it occurs today.

In addition, Tocqueville and Rousseau strongly argue that custom and tradition guide law and civil institutions, and not vice versa. In other words, both democratic theorists were acutely aware that a history and practice of democracy were more essential than any democratic structure. Present-day Russia epitomizes this point. Robert Putnam repeats this same message in his study of Italian democracy. Simply, the foundation of democracy evolves from the citizens, not from any one particular design. While we commonly hear today that America is too individualistic, born from a consuming and materialistic culture, we also find merit in the liberty that creates such individualism. In the end, the error of today's civic debate plays to America's weakness: our cautious self-analysis and our restricted initiative. We worry about our civic life. We hear of our social ills and believe they mark a downturn of American's strength of character. However, just as with Tocqueville's understanding of individualism, and as with the fine balance between liberty and equality, America's weakness is also America's greatest strength. For in our continual examination, we question our traditions and our possible futures. In America's self-understanding, we assess our social contract with our government, and lately in increasing volume, we question our economic system. In our seemingly insignificant daily actions, we confront the obstacles of modernity and money. In our practices, we surpass our theories, and today our democratic actions belie the rhetoric of civic malaise. Best of all, we know that constitutions do not save us. Instead, only our cautious, conflictual worries and concerted efforts direct us to our democratic covenant.

PRACTICE AS THEORY

Aristotle argues that the good life is one of individual flourishing. But flourishing is not simply a state ascribed. Rather, actions create an individual's flourishing, and thus happiness. Intellectual pursuits coupled with social interaction provide the basis for these actions. For democracy in particular, only when citizens directly run political affairs does flourishing emanate from the population. The import is that practice is essential to democracy, individual happiness, and the theoretical construct itself. Moreover, while practice and theory conjoin, it is practice that must meet a theoretical standard. Flourishing meets the standard for the good life, for the life worth living.

Aristotle's value comes when we contrast his democratic ideas with Michael Gross's contemporary understanding of political morality. Gross is equally concerned with human flourishing, but Gross views today's political actions and seeks to lower our democratic standards. He argues that the weak political morality underlying American representative democracy benefits society much more than its alternative—a strong democratic morality. For Gross, strong democracy posits a view of the citizen as incompatible with contemporary practice, and thus its vision and standard do not afford a realistic ethical component upon which to engage politically. Specifically, Gross states:

> Weak political morality offers a morally myopic but practically astute political actor, keenly aware of his own self-interest and cognizant of the competitive dynamics of the political order. Unlike the strong models intimated by Locke . . . , democratic society is only as strong as its structural checks and balances. There is no firm moral backstop. Self-interest, majoritarian tyranny and political corruption can get the better of even the most elaborate safeguards. . . . Weak political morality, to be fully consistent with its psychological foundations, must give up any claim to potentiality or expansive civic virtue.[4]

Whereas Tocqueville and Rousseau argue that democratic design is ineffectual without democratic customs and habits, Gross believes structure guides behavior. Get the design right, and democracy succeeds. But he states that the correct design is not one that invokes the common good and altruistic behavior. Gross sees the benefits of weak political morality because it holds a more accurate description of today's political action and political actors. He argues:

> It is no wonder that adherents of many diverse and incompatible schools of political thought find refuge in citizens who actively embrace the dictates of strong political morality. These citizens are morally sophisticated, endowed with a clear vision of ethical principles, free of sectarian interests, cognizant of the vagaries of the political environment, and capable of fierce and effective political action. Psychologically, these individuals are identified as post-conventional moral thinkers, philosophically they are morally autonomous, and socially they are unencumbered—impervious to parochial interests. . . . Each of these traits is operationalized

to answer a single question: "How effective a political actor is the liberal version of the ideal citizen?" The answer is "not very effective." . . . This reaffirms the central paradox of political morality: *The most politically competent individuals are most often the least morally competent.*[5]

Gross's problem is not with today's political behavior, but with the strong morality theory that attracts adherents to its supposed unrealistic standards. He believes that what defines political behavior today, and thus what grants society some measure of morality, is the parochial intermingling of factious interests. Whereas strong political morality casts a cosmopolitan, above-the-fray attitude, the pursuit of narrow self-interests guides most of real political action. In turn, his analysis points to guiding America's educational mission away from the altruism of civic virtue and the public good. Rather, if politics is best characterized as a match of selfish morality, then political efficacy must be the guidepost for public action. Thus, he calls for an education of the ends justifying the means simply because it appears that this is the way politics plays today.

However, two significant problems undermine Gross's views. The first is that he erroneously defines strong political morality. If strong political morality is acting beyond mere self-interest, Gross argues that this is simply not how political actors behave today. He is adverse to strong political morality because it does not capture political reality. But it is Gross's simple definitional dichotomies between parochial and independent thinking; between self-interest and the public good; and between narrow, sectarian beliefs and broad, unencumbered views that do injustice to political attitudes and actions in general. Citizens act in politics with self-interest and for the public good. At times, it is difficult to decide when which motivation takes precedence. Thus, a more complex—and thus more accurate—definition of political action and morality must weigh both strong and weak versions in concert. Sometimes citizens are altruistic and other times selfish. Sometimes, they act with both motivations. For example, in his analysis of Jewish rescue during the Holocaust, Gross demarcates parochial from post-material motivations. While the former involve material renumeration and social norms, the latter involve a sense of social responsibility and protecting basic rights. My question is, How can we distinguish the two categories? People have both motivations in mind when acting, especially when acting during the Holocaust. In this case, as in the case of the Underground Railroad in American history, I venture to argue that citizens acted not just for payment of some kind, but also for the altruistic reason of aiding or protecting other human beings.

In fact, the value of America's founding period is that the founders did not dismiss the importance of strong political morality. Rather, they designed an institutional structure of dispersed power that would check faction in order for reason and the collective will to at last emerge from the balance of parochial expression. A different understanding is that dispersed governmental authority would be controlled by a strong democratic society. Where was this strong political morality if not in the design of the government? For the founders and for Tocqueville, it was in the free interaction of civil society away from government. Gross's study highlights the necessary balance between the expression of self-interest and a concern for the common good that informs any democratic society. By noting the preponderance of morally questionable and decidedly self-interested motivations behind today's political action, he simply gives credence to the profound importance of civic groups in ensuring the common good. In essence, for democratic society not to reduce itself to a Hobbesian war of self-interest against self-interest, an active civic culture must exist. Gross certainly would agree, yet his remedy seeks not to bolster civic society, which is today's most common refrain. Instead, he accepts our moral and political condition as is, and thus seeks to change not our actions but our theoretical expectations about who participates and why they participate in democratic action.

A second problem that emerges from Gross's research is his willing acceptance of a moral standard based on so-called empirical findings from relatively recent case studies. In effect, he bases his political morality on contemporary social conditions. Thus, while he argues for a weak political morality, he does not recognize that an existing capitalistic culture and the preference for self-interested action preclude other possible moral choices. Gross's conclusion, then, seems tautological. He states that a weak political morality, which allows for parochial self-interest to guide political action, must be our preference simply because this is how political actors most often act. With little concern for the conditionality of his cases, he infers that because the evidence points to self-interested action, we need to change our theoretical understanding of political action. No need to change our actions, just our theoretical standards. He believes the theoretical standard of a broadly thinking, unencumbered citizen is simply an idealistic fallacy. But as communitarians and Lasch argue, it is precisely this unencumbered view of liberal citizenship that constitutes most of today's behavior.[6] While communitarians call for a theoretical construct that emphasizes—along with citizens who display—greater embedded ties to their communities, the value in Gross's research is that he finds just such local, immediate behavior occurring. What is not of value in Gross's research is that he is willing to discard civic virtue and common willing as utopian standards.

Aristotle understood that only through practice do individuals and citizens develop. For Gross, citizenship is the pragmatic pursuit of self-interest. This is far removed from what Aristotle meant when he said man is a social animal, and even farther removed from his ethics of moderation and tending toward the mean in behavior. A flourishing life involves more than the simple satisfaction of immediate interests. Gross, in comparison, presents a debased understanding of democratic government and social interaction. In a sense, Aristotle would argue that Gross's explanation of the practice of citizenship is not in agreement with a flourishing life or politics. While Aristotle would explain that citizenship needs less self-interest, Gross argues that what needs to be changed is our theoretical understanding of what morality and citizenship entails. Thus, Gross's apparent strawman and Aristotle's ideas bring us to an ageless query. Is it our practices that need alteration, with greater calls for civic virtue and the common good, or do we need to rethink our theories about politics and society given our selfish natures and political motivations?

PRACTICAL ALTERNATIVES

In contrast to Gross's examples, Daniel Kemmis explores a personal case that highlights both self-interest and selflessness in the public arena. In turn, Kemmis's example reveals the inadequacy of Gross's ideas. For, in contrast to Gross's fundamental thesis about the lack of political morality in the public arena, the following example displays not only selflessness and moral behavior, but also how the developmental effects of others' public morality occurs when a valuable project captures citizen interest.

Kemmis, as Missoula, Montana's mayor, was confronted with a divisive issue over the expenditure of public funds. A local group proposed to open a public-funded laundromat, the profits from which would go toward building and servicing a solar greenhouse. The greenhouse was proposed by the Down Home Project to provide work and food for several groups of disadvantaged citizens, including the developmentally disabled, the elderly, and the unemployed. However, laundromat owners throughout the city soon protested the idea that public funds were going to be spent on what they considered to be a competitor. Kemmis was asked to moderate at a meeting between the conflicting, self-interested sides. His report, at length, states:

The tension around the table at the Elks Club that evening was thick enough to float a horseshoe. These people did not understand, like, or trust each other. . . . After Wall-MacLane (director of the Down Home Project) explained what the project was all about, I asked the laundromat owners to say why they were upset. Their reason was not surprising: they didn't want public funds to be used to build a competing laundromat. . . . Once that case had been clearly made, one of the more outspoken owners turned to me and said, "Now, you've been in the legislature; you're part of government; what do you think about this?" . . . I insisted, however, that the question was not what I thought, but what the Down Home people thought. The owners were not very satisfied with that response, but they did turn their attention back to Wall-MacLane. . . .

He said, with obvious sincerity, that he understood their concern about unfair competition and wanted to be responsive to it, but that he also wanted them to understand his dilemma. . . . Finally, Wall-MacLane simply acknowledged that the arguments of the owners were sound and said that, while he thought he could hold enough votes on the city council, he could not *in good conscience* go forward with the proposal. . . .

Now clearly taken aback, the laundromat owners began trying to think of alternate ways for Down Home to generate income or *to think of ways they could support* the project. Several of them said that the city itself should support such projects, even if it meant somewhat higher taxes. . . . As the meeting broke up, one of the owners came to me and said, "*I never felt worse about winning in my life.*"[7]

In direct refutation of Gross's thesis, the fundamental change in this expression of political self-interest is the public display of morality, of *a good conscience*. After this display, the tone and perspective of the once acrimonious competitors evolved into community members resolving several collective issues with insights that extend far beyond self-interest. In this case, strong political morality—by seeing the interest of others, by being broad-minded, and by displaying independent, non-parochial thinking—changed the focus of the meeting from whether the project demands public support to the new focus of how to ensure the project's support. The show of strong political morality, so typically foreign to America's self-interested politics, turned adversaries in a winner-take-all battle into advocates for community issues.

Gross examines the abortion debate to reiterate his thesis that political actors exhibit questionable moral standards if the arena is one of political self-interest. As a counter-example, Jean Bethke Elshtain understands the abortion issue from another perspective. She argues:

All the cultural questions that now pit democratic citizens against one another—in addition to abortion, I think of family values, drugs, and post-civil rights race relations—are guaranteed to continue to divide us, in large part because of the means government has often used to put these issues on the table: judicial fiat. The Supreme Court decision in the deeply contentious *Roe v. Wade* case in 1973 actually preempted a nationwide political debate over abortion, then raging in most states. A grass-roots politics to liberalize abortion laws was well under way. Indeed, some sixteen states had already reformed their abortion statutes to make abortion more widely available. In addition, as historian Michael Barone has pointed out, "by the time the *Roe v. Wade* decision was issued, about 70% of the nation's population lived within 100 miles—an easy two hours' drive—of a state with a legalized abortion law." And just as the Supreme Court was speaking, legislatures in almost all of the states were going into session; many would probably have liberalized their abortion laws if the court had not acted. Regardless of one's personal views on abortion, this case is a good example of juridical moves freezing out citizen debate. . . . The juridical model of politics, first pushed by liberal activists and now embraced by their conservative counterparts—for two can play at this game—preempts democratic contestation and a politics of melioration.[8]

Elshtain's analysis reveals two essential points. First, the *Roe v. Wade* decision never allowed political morality to express itself. The judicial act stunted the ability of the citizenry to debate fully the fundamental questions involved. Thus, Gross's example of the abortion question as further evidence of the importance of weak political morality and self-interested politics fails in Elshtain's analysis because the entire issue was never allowed a true public airing.

Second, and directly related to Kemmis's example, Elshtain abhors this preemptive quality of today's politics because it dissuades the appropriate and necessary citizen input into democratic politics. As Kemmis shunned his badge of governmental authority when citizens sought a resolution, Elshtain infers that governmental action guides too much of today's politics. This directly relates to the individual citizen's search for meaning—and the search for certainty in an uncertain world—by looking for answers and direction from sources that ultimately leech power away from citizens in particular and from democracy in general. Again, the contentiousness and seemingly intractable political world demands citizen time, citizen thought, and most of all, citizen practice. Contrast this democratic world of action and involvement with the modern structures of bureaucratic administration—Elshtain's juridical model of politics—and social forces like television and the incongruities are obvious. Our politics demands more from us than what we have come to believe or accept. This simple idea underscores Gross's misreading of political morality as it encourages us to search for those actions that develop and sustain our democratic abilities.

Fortunately, the search demands only that we step out our front doors. Examples of citizen practice, of an active civic life, and of strong political morality inform American democracy from inner-city ghetto to suburban neighborhood. Pam Solo and Gail Pressberg give numerous examples of citizen politics that start with good ideas and demand strong moral standards, all the while ensuring America as the epitome of civic activity and homespun democratic politics. As examples, Solo and Pressberg cite a host of services that have evolved from the initiative of individuals, sometimes surmounting difficult odds, to offer valuable information for their communities. The Family Support Network in Bothell, Washington, is one such information service that unites families in crisis with active community members. Another example is The Ten Point Coalition, which is a group of African-American ministers committed to helping children under extreme pressure or who exhibit the most delinquent behavior in communities across the country. They confront gangs, monitor the streets, and provide better role models for these at-risk youth. Yet another example is the Harlem Justice Center, which is comprised of former inmates who interact in recreation programs with the most hostile kids in communities. The center's goal is to ward the kids against the possibility of a criminal future. Finally, To Market, To Market is a program that locates underrepresented and poor women and teaches them to sell specific goods, which encourages their participation in the marketplace.[9]

What is most apparent from Solo and Pressberg's list? Is it that the practice of citizenship and a vibrant civic life is alive and well in America, or is it that their examples point to civic life springing from the most economically-depressed and the most dangerous areas of society? Just as Nicholas Lemann noticed that civic virtue seems most deficient in the cities where work consumes all of people's energies, like in university towns and state and national capitals, these authors also argue that what is most missing in our civic debate is its accurate portrayal. Solo and Pressberg claim:

> Our work at the Institute for Civil Society (ICS) has allowed us a privileged view of civil society in action, and we have found that in most communities across the United States, the political philosophies of both liberals and conservatives simply miss the rich, nuanced, and complex ways in which average Americans balance the needs of communities with the needs of individuals. . . . [T]he ostensible divisiveness in public life has occurred largely at rarefied levels, among the elite members of the press corps and between opposing political camps. . . . A vibrant and lively civil society flourishes in spite of the contentious, often rancorous, public discourse.[10]

With this information, could it be that today's civic virtue debate is illusionary and masks other issues or political platforms? Since Republicans, with the Religious Right's backing, speak most often about the loss of traditional values and morality in society, is this debate a conservative initiative to focus attention away from economic practices and social inequalities? I have at least alluded to as much. But Solo and Pressberg also implicate liberals for being equally inept at witnessing the diversity and value of the civic groups that do exist. In spite of the injustices of the capitalist economy and the maddening forces that stifle human initiative and creativity, civic groups like the inner-city church have maintained and created sources of support to overcome the social ills that beset their communities. Certainly many fight an uphill battle, but without them, glimmers of hope turn quickly into despair. The message, then, is not that American civic life is dead or dying. Rather, civic life not only exists beyond where traditionally it has occurred, from the tradition of the Elks Club to today's kids' soccer fields, but it also occurs beyond our traditional labeling mechanisms, from the traditions of Right and Left to today's nonpartisan, community-oriented activities. Thus, in updating Tocqueville's view of American democracy, where we most fail is not in our civic activities but in understanding where they exist and why they exist where they do.

Also, it is especially apt that Solo and Pressberg employ the word *flourishes* in the above quotation. For, in the Aristotlean sense, where civic life exists, lives truly flourish. This means that the apparent divide between lives lived by social and political elites who lament the loss of associational life and social capital, and the rest of America spells out the true, underlying difference in our civic culture. The issue, then, turns from broad social problems that envelop America to a specific malaise that signifies the lack of social interaction from America's privileged classes. As Christopher Lasch argues, what appears most lacking is the social connections the advantaged have to their communities' issues. While what we hear from the media is that America's civic life has diminished, the more descriptive alternative may be that society's advantaged feel a sense of disillusionment and despair stemming from their increasing distance from their communities. As they embrace the privileges of the global marketplace, they also lose the strong ties that come from neighborhood meetings and public school functions. What they have forsaken is what Aristotle and all other democratic theorists demand from the citizens: the ongoing practice of not just governing but interacting over common issues by the individuals who make up the polity. Today's civic debate may reveal the simple fact that work life and leisure pursuits cannot constitute all of the country's activities. It should be obvious if not tautological that civic life emerges from citizens' flourishing practices of participation.

AMERICA'S THEORY FOR CIVIC LIFE

While the notion of practice appeals to our civic sentiments, Aristotle's teleological view of human nature, in that we are pre-wired to pursue specific human ends, carries only so much power these days. Aristotle's good life of the requisite combination of reason and virtue can be achieved only by a select few, as he views merchants and work of any kind antithetical to attaining the end of man, or happiness. In fact, his entire theoretical construct is carried on the backs of slaves who do the work necessary for the citizenry to concern itself with personal and civic ends. America today is simply too democratic for Aristotle's model, as we extend suffrage and citizenship more broadly than he imagined. However, the question that arises is have we compromised this model of ongoing practice if we necessitate economic activity, family obligations, and child-rearing in addition to the duties of civic engagement? Conversely, does citizenship carry any value when people must also meet the expectations of making a living, ensuring their futures, and providing for others? These questions return us to the mire of modern living and the difficulty of developing a public attitude and a civic commitment while also satisfying personal and familial obligations.

Theories that appear impossible to practice are more the norm than the exception. Jean-Jacques Rousseau's participatory ideas receive this treatment. His theory of citizens representing their own interests in public legislatures and the preeminence of the general will over any partial interest seems especially apt for America's civic debate today. But critics focus on the issues of scale and on the unexamined necessity of prior agreement— to maintain allegiance to the social union when one is in disagreement with its views and policies—in denouncing Rousseau's model of participatory democracy. Interestingly, though, Rousseau's ideas should appeal to conservatives today as his republic espouses several of the same themes heard from today's Right. Along with his perceptive transformation of individual independence to collective allegiance, which favors the interests of the majority over those of the individual, Rousseau also advocated a civil religion.[11] Throughout his thinking, his intention was to create institutions or lasting social bonds that would foster unity and collective cohesion. From our earlier discussion, Rousseau believed the good preceded and was much more important than rights. Citizens maintained rights, but those rights were dependent upon the general will. Unfortunately, a national religion is often cited as Rousseau's undoing. But given the power of the Religious Right today, coupled with the growth of groups like the Promise Keepers and the Baptist reiteration of women's subservient place in the home, it seems that today's conservative declarations can find significant agreement in Rousseau's social contract.

If Aristotle and Rousseau's ideas seem not just outdated but filled with anti-democratic ideas, like the need for a single, national religion, then most often today's democrats turn not to Tocqueville, as his ideas also fit well in the conservative camp, but to Jefferson. Jefferson offers a participatory alternative that counters the distance modern, big government politics displays. He develops a small-scale system that appears reasonable if we begin to recognize where it is that we most often practice politics. He also offers an anti-corporate view that follows some of today's thinking. Most importantly, though, Jefferson's ideas give preeminence to the value and worth of citizens in deciding for themselves how to govern. As opposed to most of the Federalists in his time, Jefferson places great respect in the ability of citizens to run the country. As Richard K. Matthews summarizes:

Jefferson's political system specifically calls for mass participatory democracy. He advocates a pyramid structure of government in which each higher level is held directly and immediately accountable to its next lower level. Politics, furthermore, is to become a daily part of human life; no longer will it be a biennial, momentary fulfillment of a duty. . . . [Participation] is also a constant check against tyranny and an additional avenue in which men can pursue happiness. Freedom also requires each generation must have the chance to begin society over again; every twenty years, all the laws would automatically become void. Laws are not "sanctimonious"; they have to be rewritten to suit the change in circumstances as well as men. Jefferson's open-ended political philosophy actively encourages individuals . . . to create and re-create community. These celebrations of democratic community, moreover, simultaneously provide a good opportunity to redistribute property, thereby protecting an individual's economic independence. They also keep the society in a state of constant revolution, in harmony with human and social evolution. Participatory democracy in both the political realm and the economic realm is, to Jefferson, a necessary prerequisite to human fulfillment.[12]

There appears much to change and much to fear perhaps if Jefferson's ideas are taken seriously. First and foremost, though, his ideas of constant revolution are less dangerous than they appear. His intent is to maintain not just a spirit of national union and identity, but also he seeks to sustain what he sees as the human desire to gather new information, create new ideas, build new constructs, and experiment in life. In essence, he views the human spirit as one that thrives on change, interaction, and creation. This spirit of invention and change necessitates the continual examination of both personal and collective issues. If given the opportunity, this collective examination would satisfy the need for human creation as well as building a formidable collective identity. In fact, it is precisely the lack of any collective unity that underscores today's civic virtue debate. Jefferson attempts to redress this issue by demanding generational change and ongoing input from all citizens.

The basic political structure is the ward, and Jefferson's demand for citizen participation follows his acerbic review of the federal design of America's government. He states:

> In the legislature, the House of Representatives [of Virginia] is chosen by less than half the people, and not at all in proportion to those who do choose. The Senate are still more disproportionate, and for long terms of irresponsibility . . . where then is our republicanism to be found? Not in our Constitution certainly, but merely in the spirit of our people. . . . Divide the counties into wards of such size as that every citizen can attend, when called on, and act in person. Ascribe to them the government of their wards in all things relating to themselves exclusively. . . . We should thus marshal our government into, one, the general federal republic; two, that of the State, for what relates to our own citizens exclusively; three, the county republics, for the duties and concerns of the county; and four, the ward republics, for the small, and yet numerous and interesting concerns of the neighborhood. . . . And the whole is cemented by giving to every citizen, personally, a part in the administration of the public affairs.[13]

Of course, the demand for ward republics is a demand for citizen education. It is thus one of the foremost societal functions to educate its members into the role of citizen. In this age of doubt and cynicism about public interest, this seems a tall order. Perhaps, though, the alternative view is that if America had a history of citizen education, of citizen involvement with each individual's necessary inclusion in the political process, then this demand today would seem customary and not foolhardy—a politics by everyone who reduces the privileges associated with today's politics. If a learning curve is necessary, then government's role would be to create support agencies to initiate the population. Appeals for term limits would be satisfied by design. But of the greatest importance, it is not a significant leap from America's active associational life today, with its moral compass, to Jefferson's ward republics. The issues and scale remain the same, only that by design everyone expresses a public voice. In turn, unity forms and human creativity flourishes.

Moreover, what Jefferson offers is democratic politics as it needs to be:

active, ongoing, and inventive. Interestingly Jefferson offers a politics that places power not in a constitutional design, but in the citizens themselves to collectively design government and politics as they envision. A Jeffersonian politics cannot be easily categorized as the people choose how they form collective decisions. Certainly, traditions will evolve that will provide continuity, but when power resides away from any national capital and away from a definitive constitutional form, then democracy becomes regenerative with constant creative initiative. Benjamin Barber captures the conjoining of theory and practice in Jeffersonian politics when he summarizes that

> Democrats and egalitarians owe him [Jefferson] a debt less as a "founder" than as a devotee of an antifoundationalist participatory politics of the present and the future that allowed what might have become a stultifying system of stasis to become a revolutionary instrument each new generation of Americans might employ in their own struggle for enfranchisement and rights. In short, it is not so much Jefferson's principles in the Declaration but the practical politics and civic education those principles justified to which egalitarians ought to pay tribute. The critics have called his integrity into question by contrasting his principles with his practices as a slaveholder—but the whole point of the principles in question was to subject all principles to constant criticism. Jefferson is important to modern democrats because he expounds the most essential (and paradoxical) of all democratic principles: that politics always trumps principle. In the short term, this may dismay upholders of the "right" principle (such as the principles of right). But in the long run, it is the only hope for both principles and for rights.[14]

As a thought experiment, if Jefferson's ideas were in place, would the existence of a healthy civic life be a hotly debated topic? Our civic life would be an essential element of our daily lives. It would not be captured by others, nor would it exclude as many as it does today. Government's role would be as much to inform the public as it would be to serve its interests. Thus, the power of Jefferson's approach is that he allows the citizenry's democratic practice to be its theory. But in contrast to Barber's interpretation, by no means is Jefferson's approach nonfoundational. It is only that the foundation of a democratic politics remains invested in the citizenry, with the citizenry deciding how to proceed. Certainly, this century has witnessed the importance of securing individual rights—often against an oppressive, sometimes racist majority—but perhaps a more inclusive politics would produce more democratic commitments and results. In a sense, then, when we view America's civic associations today, it is very much the first step toward defining a Jeffersonian political theory.

FROM THEORY TO TODAY'S CIVIC ACTION:
THE SOURCES OF CHANGE

Yet, with my call for a politics in the Jeffersonian tradition, what would such a politics look like? My call is only a repetition of numerous other invocations of Jefferson's legacy. If so many authors, community activists, political researchers, and social commentators find answers to today's problems in Jefferson's ideas, why does America suffer from a lack of political participation and civic interest? Is it simply that we do not heed our own advice? Are Jefferson's ideas a democratic utopia? Or, are there too many entrenched interests in today's political processes, and while we call for a more involved citizenry, is it precisely an involved citizenry that adds greater uncertainty to today's invested powers?

To answer these questions, we need to understand the social changes that underlie today's political questioning. It is my argument that any return to some watershed civic era discounts the value of social change, and that civic activity that ushers in the importance of, say, fraternal organizations, misses the value present society does or does not grant these organiza-tions. In short, any change today must work in concert with the social changes Americans have come to accept. Thus, to energize political life demands not revolutionary change, but mere additions to the civic life that already flourishes. As William Galston and Peter Levine describe today's group or civic life, we can infer the minor extent of change necessary. They note that almost half the population engages in church-related groups, and that these affiliations have direct links to more obvious forms of political participation such as voting and volunteering. Although "mail-order" groups have blossomed since the 1970s, they warn against the common labeling that these groups are truly not associational. In some instances, they remain strictly tied to money, with little or no interaction. But examples exist of strong community involvement, as the Sierra Club epitomizes. Galston and Levine argue:

> The evidence now available does not permit firm conclusions about the overall condition of associational life in America. But it does seem that voluntary activities are on balance healthier than are formal political institutions and processes. In-deed, citizens, particularly the youngest, seem to be shifting their preferred civic involvement from official politics to the voluntary sector. If so, the classic Tocquevillian thesis would have to be modified: local civic life, far from acting as a school for wider political involvement, may increasingly serve as a refuge from (and alternative to) it.[15]

Although Galston and Levine hesitate to draw conclusions from their research, I will not. America's political and social condition is a matter of perspective. At the national level, research shows a general contempt for politics. But at the local level, where David Mathews earlier recognized that political activity is called by other names—such as community issues, neighborhood groups, and local concerns—civic activity is broad and deep. As opposed to Robert Putnam's view that America's increase in bowler participation and its decrease in league participation reflects the more general loss of civic activity, an alternative view is that civic activity is as vibrant as ever, perhaps more vibrant given the increasing citizen awareness of the public implications. As unions and the traditional Elks, Moose, and Lions clubs have seen precipitous decreases in membership, Mothers Against Drunk Driving (MADD), Community Development Corporations (CDCs), and other regional or local groups fighting specific problems more than replace these broad-based civic relics.

But simply replacing one set of groups with another does little to address the social ills that need public attention. The chimera that is the conservative agenda placates most of us with moral posturing, ignoring how to solve social problems—is "just say no" a legitimate, serious public response to drug use and its crimes?—that spill over from the inner cities to more affluent areas. My argument that America remains as civic-minded as ever with a listing of the new civic groups that have emerged over the last ten to twenty years provides little understanding of the social changes that necessitate this new civic awareness. New civic groups are no longer filled with the traditional cross-class American Legions, Knights of Columbus, and Moose Club members. New groups tend to respond to pressing social issues, such as rampant crime rates in the inner cities. The conviviality that marked these older civic methods has been replaced with a dire urgency to check raging problems. The call that needs trumpeting is not a restoration of American civic life. Rather, the call is for greater collective attention to the social ills that demand our continued civic activity.

To state that our civic life is alive and well does not diminish the seriousness of current social problems that demand Jeffersonian commitment. To revisit my earlier economic argument, America's civic life reflects the profound changes in America's economic and social conditions. The movement away from traditional fraternal organizations toward civic groups more actively involved in solving immediate concerns epitomizes the increasing income and wealth differentials in society and the attendant problems that arise from egregious economic inequality. The halcyon days that permitted bankers and teachers, merchants and service people, and real estate agents and clergymen to find common time to discuss public concerns has been lost. As Theda Skocpol notes, "Better educated Americans, in short, have pulled out of broad community groups in record numbers since the mid-1970s, sometimes leaving behind people with high school educations or less. . . . The best educated people are still participating in more groups overall, but not in the same groups as their less well-educated fellow citizens."[16] Thus, while the veneer of civic life still shines brightly, the underside is that this lack of cross-class interaction produces pockets of different interests. It is politically obvious, too, that those less well-off have more pressing social ills to confront, more immediate challenges to the individual's safety and security, than do the more well-off. Just as suburbanization has challenged America's approach to race, urban politics, and welfare issues, civic activity is another example of fundamental economic and social differences in American society.

Furthermore, to return to Putnam's bowling example, perhaps the decrease in league participation is fueled by economic insecurity. Mom and Dad no longer bowl together—or bowl on separate nights—because one of them needs to baby-sit the kids while the other works a second job or a double shift. Civic life is compromised when providing the necessities becomes an uncertainty, or when it becomes an entire day's object, stretching out far beyond an eight-hour workday. If the middle class feels an economic squeeze, the growing underclasses feel the tightening vise grip of poverty, poorer health, and greater danger in their daily lives. In turn, while neighborhood watch groups monitor surburban toddlers, inner-city neighborhoods must cope with inferior educational facilities and opportunities, and the street life of drugs and crime. Often, the community members themselves put up the fight, as the police cannot act quickly enough. Through it all, the local church is often the only ray of refuge and hope.

The central concern for America's civic health is not its demise. Instead, Americans need to focus on how different classes or, if we are uneasy about the concept of class in America, how different segments in society express their civic virtue. In this light, perhaps government does need to play a smaller role in the life of surburbia, as those citizens are better capable of meeting their needs. Government, then, can focus its attention on more complex, more demanding civic areas. This bias offends some, but the preferential action finds just reasoning when we make a comprehensive cost-benefit calculation for society as a whole. It also is just simply based on democratic principles of inclusion and opportunity. In the end, after the much noted growing inequality that grips American society, it seems reasonable to expect that America's civic life also would mirror this growing inequality. If our civic health remains as robust as the numbers indicate, then it is certain that the civic life for a professional management worker involves distinct organizations and commitments, which is not true for a lower class blue-collar worker who first needs to make ends meet.

Skocpol identifies another worthy civic distinction. She notes that along with the wealthy opting out of cross-class organizations, fewer associations tie local groups to national organizations. She observes that "there has been a 'missing middle' in all this recent associational proliferation— an absence of links from national to local groups. With several notable exceptions, such as the Christian Coalition, few new local-state-national federations have been founded since the 1960s and 1970s. And many of the thirty to forty nationwide voluntary federations that flourished in mid-twentieth-century America have gone into absolute as well as relative membership decline."[17] Again, economic changes help foster these missing links. As women enter the workforce and as America develops a highly-skilled professional class, people have favored those groups that satisfy their work interests or advance their careers. To rise up the ladder in a professional career may in fact mean giving time to the state or national organization representing one's work field. In turn, the civic life that falls by the wayside is the local community issues. While the professionals simply move from undesirable locations, they leave little behind: less tax money, fewer educational resources, and less public concern.

Thus, the question is not whether America's civic life exists, but how its civic life is different in its various communities. In more affluent areas, where security is less a concern, civic life involves the interaction of school concerns, local business development, and tax issues. In more troubled areas, schooling remains a central focus, but the questions are not, "How dow we tackle this issue?" Rather, they are, "Can we or is it possible to address this?" The difference is the degree of both community and monetary support. In the end, economic changes fuel the civic malaise from all class perspectives. The affluent focus on building a professional career to the exclusion of their local civic issues. They lose a sense of connection to a locale and its history. The poor or underclasses rely on strong local leaders and institutions to help rectify their changing economic conditions. They lose a sense of connection to their neighborhoods when they deteriorate before their eyes. The middle classes feel an economic pinch these days, and while they recognize the importance of community involvement, it may be one area in which they must participate less in order to pay bills and care for their children.

Before I leave this topic, I think it important to point out that our understanding of civic life may also reflect a methodological bias. It appears much easier to measure national organizations and national attitudes about

America's civic life than it is to accumulate disparate examples of citizen activity throughout the country. Only after exhaustive research, combing city after town and county after crossroads, can we begin to assess the depth of civic involvement. Perhaps previous research methods mirrored the accessibility of the traditional fraternal organizations. It was simple to count the membership rolls from all the Elks Club or Rotary Club meetings across the country. Today, however, as a reflection of the increasing specialization in society, groups committed to narrowly-defined interests have multiplied. Their civic intent is at times difficult to gauge, as is their connection with other groups and interests.

It appears that a traditional bias is built into social science research, and the study of civic life must change just as the expression of civic life has changed. In turn, perhaps more detailed, more encompassing research can reveal informative analyses and not simply the hand-wringing and moral platitudes that often strangle America's national discussion about its changing, not declining, civic activities.

OUR CIVIC (COM)PROMISE

To recognize that communities differ in their civic associations does not provide much insight. To understand that civic activities are a sign of civic health and community wealth adds a bit more perspective. Finally, to realize that the economic wealth and social health of a community determine the kinds of civic activities that people create and the types of groups to which they will flock seems patently obvious. Civic differentiation—the idea that poorer communities will need to rely perhaps on church charity and government assistance more than richer locales that can raise funds independently—seems an important distinction to note. Rarely in the discussion of America's civic health is this differentiation emphasized. In general, civic activity is viewed as an amalgamation of diverse groups, but all with similar effects: the promotion of a public spirit and the inculcation of unity, togetherness, and shared efforts for larger goals.

Civic differentiation, though, demands a sharper focus of what and why civic activities function where they do. Also, with civic differentiation comes the demand for a clarity of supportive aid to those communities under the most duress. In this sense, justice arises from the actions to help those most in need. The relative importance of the suburban groups that band together to fight a sales tax increase pales in comparison to the assistance necessary for an inner-city church to provide a safe haven and drug-free initiatives for its local youth. Yet, both are signs of civic activity. My only point here is to understand the priority of the latter, and thus the need for public and governmental support if we are to fulfill a politics of citizen interest and involvement. For, ultimately, we need to address whether a broad chasm exists between a Jeffersonian politics—which demands ongoing citizen participation and an inclusive involvement of all of society's members— and a society of civic differentiation?

Understanding civic differentiation is not necessarily a condemnation of suburbia or elite enclaves. If a pointed message exists, it is that many absolve themselves by not giving their participation, insights, and resources to address issues that affect the broader communities outside of their sheltered, or perhaps gated, neighborhoods. A Jeffersonian project calls for all to interact for the common good. The hope and expectation is that the power of improvement lies with the people, not with government or with corporate appeasement. Also, understanding civic differentiation is not a search for a common, national identity. America's project in the twentieth century—emanating from the warnings of Dewey and Lippman about modern bureaucracy and corporate businesses sapping the vitality from America's home-spun, small-town vitality—has been the search for a national community. From Teddy Roosevelt's call for a stronger national government to the 1960s' New Frontier and Great Society initiatives, William A. Schambra states that America has sought to maintain and encourage a sense of community even as its small-town, neighborly traditions became historical relics. Today, however, in true Jeffersonian spirit, Schambra believes that a national community is a meaningless objective. He argues, instead, that a more individualized focus needs recognition and support, as the national organizations seemingly have given up the social fight and now simply resign themselves to protecting their narrow interests. Schambra observes:

Yet to our elites, these grass-roots initiatives are invisible, or if visible, dismissed as charismatic exceptions or inspiring but isolated anecdotes. After all, they're not docile subsidiaries of the larger, "acceptable" nonprofits, but rather scrappy, scruffy, fiercely independent local initiatives, too busy working with the poor to join coalitions against poverty. They are not staffed by credentialed bureaucrats, but by volunteers whose chief credential may be that they themselves have only recently overcome the daunting circumstances of the inner city. . . . We should also highlight the ways in which private and public resources can be redirected to those who have already accomplished so much with virtually no outside help at all. Here the federal government should have a role too—not as grand builder of national community, but as humble servant to the genuine community builders within our neighborhoods.[18]

Again, the themes of including but managing the national government's role exists alongside the demanding, hard-fought, and unnoticed community efforts to build stronger bonds and overcome difficult social conditions. A reduced national government role allows people to express their public voice and demands that they act for the good of their communities. Reducing the scale and scope of America's sense of community allows for Jefferson's inclusive participation. But reducing the scope does not address the economic inequalities that foster the burgeoning need for citizens to act publicly. In fact, the other, more secretive explanation of why America is consumed with this civic debate today—away from the diatribe that government action feeds rather than resolves the ills of poverty, welfare, homelessness, and crime—is best understood as the heartfelt public recognition of, but its misguided remedy for, the effects of severe economic differences. Now, instead of allowing government to act on our behalf, it is up to the citizens—and not just the citizens of depressed, crime-laden areas—to solve, with government's help, these fundamental issues that strike at the core of a democratic, just society.

At America's core, justice entails the ability to live an independent life. This does not mean Tocqueville's idea of independence, of individualism wrongly understood as selfishness. Instead, it is Jefferson's concept of the hearty ability to provide for oneself and one's family. As Richard Matthews notes:

[For Jefferson,] there is no natural right to property; such rights are social grants, created to aid men in the pursuit of life, liberty, and happiness. . . . While the accumulation of property is not the essence of humanity, a sufficient amount of it is necessary in order to guarantee individual freedom. . . . To ensure further economic as well as political freedom, Jefferson advances his principle that the "Earth Belongs to the Living." . . . [In the end,] Jefferson is arguing for a right to a particular style of life, a life from which men have a right not to be excluded. . . . [T]he mentality of Jefferson's world view, the ethos that composes and pervades it, brings to the fore a different dimension (than other radical bourgeois theories) in his particular brand of radical thought: aesthetic experiences, friendship, community, felicity, leisure—not profitability—are the controlling concerns of this vision.[19]

It is precisely the exercise in community that counters the dangers of market individualism and the preeminence of property and economic measures. Jefferson, then, reminds us, and Tocqueville would soon repeat him, that the inequality that economic relations produce hinder the ability of people to practice democracy. Today's civic debate seems an expression, albeit perverted expression at times, of this age-old observation.

Yet again we recognize the duality inherent in America's social condition. For it is true that civic life flourishes, and does so in the most inhumane situations, across this country. In fact, civic life is the Jeffersonian recognition that average, everyday people have the ability to govern their communities and express their heartfelt interests. However, citizen action often represents a last defense against losing all faith to the ills of crime, drugs, unemployment, "redlining," corporate whims, and poverty. Instead of proactively granting citizens control of their communities and their individual lives, often public policies hinder citizens' abilities. The covenant of citizen government is most often compromised by those institutions we accept to act on our behalf to fulfill this covenant. Government retains a questionable and contentious role these days, at some times as a mechanism for aid and other times as an enabler of social disaster. But while government receives the blame in shallow campaign promises and in even more shallow political rhetoric, deeper inequalities structure business, government, and society to crippling, anti-democratic injustices.

To return to the question of a possible hindrance to a Jeffersonian practical politics from the discrepancies between different types of civic behavior, we are left with an equivocal answer. The promise is that citizens do act in significant numbers to assist their neighbors, to safeguard and monitor their communities, and to build a sense of solidarity and mutual concern that epitomizes Jefferson's views. Also, we should emphasize that citizens act at times in dire situations with monumental obstacles and with little support and money. Civic virtue, then, runs the gamut from coping with the worst consequences of American society to building upon successful starts from other generations and providing safer, more viable futures for following generations. In contrast, the compromise inherent in today's civic activity is that the future varies in its promise depending upon the community where citizens live. Citizens show they have the desire and the initiative to work at the local level, a trait political research reveals is missing for national issues. The question remains whether citizens will have the opportunities to develop their interests and to apply their democratic skills to any future politics. Jefferson offers a manageable guide. Today's civic displays offer essential practice, and often in the face of long odds. Those odds, though, are increasing and demand ever more an analysis of America's democratic contract.

NOTES

1. The Tragically Hip, "Save the Planet," *Phantom Power*, Sire Records, 1998.
2. Thomas Jefferson to James Madison, 6 September 1789, *The Portable Thomas Jefferson*, ed. Merrill D. Peterson (New York: Viking Penguin, 1975), 449.
3. William A. Galston and Peter Levine, "America's Civic Condition: A Glance

at the Evidence," in *Community Works: The Revival of Civil Society in America*, ed. E. J. Dionne, Jr. (Washington, D.C.: The Brookings Institution, 1998), 31.

4. Michael L. Gross, *Ethics and Activism: The Theory and Practice of Political Morality* (New York: Cambridge University Press, 1997), 38–39.

5. Ibid., 226.

6. See Michael J. Sandel, *Democracy's Discontent: America in Search of a Public Philosophy* (Cambridge, Mass.: The Belknap Press of Harvard University Press, 1996), 11–24.

7. Daniel Kemmis, *Community and the Politics of Place* (Norman, Okla.: University of Oklahoma Press, 1990), 111–112. (Italics mine.)

8. Jean Bethke Elshtain, *Democracy on Trial* (New York: Basic Books, 1995), 26–27.

9. Pam Solo and Gail Pressberg, "Beyond Theory: Civil Society in Action," in *Community Works: The Revival of Civil Society in America*, ed. E. J. Dionne, Jr., 83–85.

10. Ibid., 83.

11. Jean-Jacques Rousseau, *The Social Contract*, trans. Maurice Cranston (New York: Penguin Books, 1968), 60, 176. (Book I, Chapter 6, and Book IV, Chapter 8).

12. Richard K. Matthews, *The Radical Politics of Thomas Jefferson: A Revisionist View* (Lawrence, Kans.: University Press of Kansas, 1984), 126.

13. Thomas Jefferson to Samuel Kercheval, 12 July 1816, *The Portable Thomas Jefferson*, ed. Merrill D. Peterson (New York: Viking Penguin, 1975), 554–557.

14. Benjamin R. Barber, "Thomas Jefferson and the Education of the Citizen," in *A Passion for Democracy: American Essays* (Princeton, N.J.: Princeton University Press, 1998), 167–168.

15. William A. Galston and Peter Levine, "America's Civic Condition," in *Community Works*, ed. E. J. Dionne, Jr., 33–34, 36.

16. Theda Skocpol, "Don't Blame Big Government: America's Voluntary Groups Thrive in a National Network," in *Community Works*, ed. E. J. Dionne, Jr., 43.

17. Ibid., 42.

18. William A. Schambra, "All Community is Local: The Key to America's Civic Renewal," in *Community Works*, ed. E. J. Dionne, Jr., 49.

19. Richard K. Matthews, *The Radical Politics of Thomas Jefferson: A Revisionist View* (Lawrence, Kans.: University of Kansas Press, 1984), 50–52.

6

~

Changing Our Balance

If nothing else, my analysis seeks to reveal the complexity of—and thus the inherent danger in generalizing about—America's civic health. A national discussion about the character and choices of American's public behavior warrants input from all social groups and political perspectives. It demands a seriousness and interest that recognizes the lasting effects of the collective decisions. Instead, too often today the debate focuses on immoral actions from the least desirable social elements. The public debate easily devolves into political posturing and safe position-taking. Tocqueville's ideas are bandied about in a well-worn and misguided manner. The tenor is that America suffers from a social and political malaise as society devolves into either increasingly isolated consumers or increasingly hostile, single-issue cynics. With its charade and clichés, to which add the confusion that the ever-similar sides level at each other as they wink out of camera view, it is little wonder Americans disown politics and politicians. In fact, citizens know that candidates simply sling mud and incumbents never offer an unequivocal stand.

Overlay the political dissent with the inherent difficulties each individual confronts in a constantly changing world. Aside from politics as usual, the immediate enigmas are the changes in everyday life. Changes this century include expansion of the franchise to women and minorities, the creation of a burgeoning federal presence to check economic excess and ensure greater social welfare protection, and the witness of the fallout from world wars and economic colonialism. This generation sees changes such as the Cold War dissipation, the globalization of markets with the simplistic view of globalizing democracy, and the mind-boggling increase in the speed of communication and access to information. The consequences for every

American are that the economy changes from a muscle-bound giant of bountiful consumer durables to a lean, post-industrial communication and service-oriented mechanism. Citizens as employees must retool and respond. New industries demand new skills. Yesterday's mechanic is lost at today's keyboard. Children make the best computer geniuses, and the best computer hackers. All the while, the VCR remains unprogrammed, that is, until the kids get home to play cyber-games. The economy now demands that both parents work, and the family as a social institution must retool too. Speed and dexterity are the necessary skills today, except at home and in the neighborhood.

Today's intellectuals, from academia and the research institutes to politicians and social commentators, most often point to the abysmal election turnouts and the significant decline in traditional civic organizations as signs of America's effete associational life. While the topics of a seething immorality and the loss of family values have cross-pollinated to both political parties, my argument is that civic life in America exists, and it is as strong, if not stronger, than it ever was. In fact, I believe America's civic life is as potent as it is today out of necessity. Americans, who are individualistic consumers on one hand, on the other hand display their Tocquevillean appellation of "joiners" seeking to redress immediate, local problems. When a town's primary industry leaves for cheaper labor markets, citizens act to mollify the social and economic devastation. When government co-opts a successful initiative or supplants local shoots of growth, or when government downsizes in the name of efficiency, citizens act to adjust to the dashed hopes and failed expectations. Citizens organize to attract business to their depressed areas. Citizens work to find meaningful spaces and events for themselves and their children. Thus, a wide rift exists between community activity and politics in general. Politics is distant and professionalized, filled with complex issues that typically are distorted beyond intelligent discussion. Community activity is neighbors and local businesspeople working for obvious collective benefits.

At one time the American barn-raising event symbolized the ties of community and the benefits of working together. However, barn-raising is a nostalgic remnant of a different time and place. In its place, we may have a desolate barn construction operation at the edge of town that a conglomerate bought and then sold as the operation failed to meet some specified profit margin. While barn-raising once granted Americans a feel-good vision about progress and working toward a brighter, more prosperous future, today's idea of community diverges from these rose-colored views when we consider the idea of civic differentiation. In the suburbs, perhaps this vision of a brighter future still glows—glows though in sub-dued hues—but in America's more depressed communities, civic action works toward safe streets, fewer drugs, more police, and less violence. Similar to Maslow's hierarchy of needs for individuals, a community must first satisfy its basic needs of safety and sustenance before it can actualize toward a future vision. When economic changes rip the suste-nance from a community's hands, its focus settles on its present, and churches, merchants, and concerned citizens find themselves forced to defend their communities or witness their extinction. When we speak of civic life, it is important to understand the difference between one era's barn-raising and another's church youth services and food drives. The former exemplifies America's past spirit while the latter reveals America's troubled present.

While civic differentiation casts a pall over the vibrancy that exudes from America's hope from and for its civic life, it begins to notice what truly ails the country, and it provides a readily apparent course of action. Tocqueville's trenchant insights hail associational life as the cornerstone for securing liberty and ensuring democracy. What aided civic life in our democracy's infancy was the relative equality Tocqueville witnessed. While he warned of equality's tyrannical possibilities, America countered equality's effects with its robust citizen interaction. America is much more politically and economically equal in comparison to early nineteenth cen-tury society, yet today we are growing less equal. The gulf widens between the rich and poor, and between the upper and the middle classes. What becomes apparent is that to solve problems in one realm, for instance the civic or social realm, demands action and change in other realms. Civil society does not function in isolation from economic and political activity. If nothing else, this recognition means that a return to a Tocquevillean ideal, or to some post-World War II unity, is simple-minded. The economy de-mands different talents and more time from Americans. Politics has been dispatched to professionals and obscured by rhetoric. To envision a more vibrant and bountiful civic life today demands more from citizens. In re-turn, to demand more citizen action necessitates a host of economic and political changes that encourage their input and enlivens the democratic experience.

NECESSARY INTER-CHANGE

The understanding that an even more robust civic life demands greater citizen action does not challenge my argument that civic life is alive and well. Obviously, many Americans work selflessly for collective benefits every day. Examples of innumerable local groups that address problems and foster change in city after city epitomize America's civic spirit. But as the idea of civic differentiation indicates, civic activity in many cases is a last-call reprieve to ward off decay and impoverishment. Civic activity is especially important in impoverished areas, and it demands government support to redress the inequalities that produce decaying neighborhoods. Furthermore, the nature of civic activity is that more is better. Generally, this is true, until functions and agendas duplicate. More groups with more ideas engender interaction and dialogue. Democracy flourishes when diverse interests intertwine. Not all interests are validated all the time, but that is part of the meliorative construction of working toward group interests and accommodating others' ideas.

The point in raising the idea of a holistic approach toward civic life is that often civil society is viewed as a realm distinct from economic and political activity. I chastise conservatives for their narrow emphasis on the decline of social mores as they fail to see the connection between viable economic opportunities and citizenship. As another example, in his latest work, Benjamin Barber, the advocate of what he labels "strong democratic" citizenship, does not state clearly the interconnectedness between economic activity, political action, and civil society. Instead, he views civil society as a separate arena that mediates between market, contractual relations—typically viewed as the private realm—and governmental activity—typically viewed as the public realm. Barber argues the paucity of civic life today comes from its emasculation from these other two arenas. Social networks, civic groups, and public works pale in relation to the size of government and its need to monitor the growth of the marketplace. Big government is the obvious result of big business. The dire result is the demise of civic action.

Barber describes America's democratic models as the option between two failing methods. One is the libertarian model, which is based on the inclusive contractual relations between autonomous individuals. Although, in the end, it leaves citizens empty and alone. A second model is the communitarian philosophy, and while it promotes a more embedded sense of citizenship, Barber argues it tends toward exclusivity. As a third model, Barber proposes his strong democratic model, which seeks to combine voluntaristic choice, inclusiveness, and a sense of connection through the intersection of private and public action. He states:

This strong democratic perspective on civil society distinguishes public and private realms—a state sector occupied by government . . . , and a private sector occupied by individuals and their contract associations in the "market"—and presumes a third domain mediating between them, sharing the virtues of each. This third, independent sector is defined by its civic communities—their plurality is its essence—which are membership associations that are open and egalitarian enough to permit voluntary participation.[1]

All these civic engagements . . . share with the private sector the gift of liberty; we go to them voluntarily and join in them as freely associated individuals and groups. But unlike private sector associations, these groups afford common ground and collaborative modes of action and have a public feel without being coercive; they permit voluntary activity that is not, however, privatized.[2]

Barber's definition seems confusing if democratic civil society is independent of the state and market realms and yet mediates between them. If it shares the virtues of each realm—that is civil society seeks both voluntary choice and inclusive design—without attacking the vices of each realm, then those vices are left to infect citizens. A more powerful definition of strong democratic citizenship seeks not to separate these three realms and allow each its own rules and relationships. Rather, a strong civic culture seeps into all activity, both private and public, and seeks to imbue the virtues of civic life into economic and government activity. For ultimately in a democratic society, citizens have the power to determine how to interact in their economic affairs and public duties. The market does not dictate a contractual emptiness and isolation, nor does governmental business demand coercive servitude. For truly civic citizens, economics and government are simply two avenues to express their ongoing concerns and interests.

Barber argues against the libertarian and communitarian approaches because they do not incorporate enough democratic attributes. The libertarian model fails for it treats the citizen only as a consumer; the communitarian model fails for it allows only for thick bonds to determine choice and action. For Barber, to offer a third model of strong democratic citizenship proposes to address the multifaceted dimensions of each citizen's personality. Including Barber's model, citizens can act as consumers in the market, as loyal subjects in government coercion, and as involved and active players in their neighborhoods and communities. But the result seems inconclusive. For Barber's strong citizenship proposes another layer of relationships, albeit essential democratic ones, to the already existing relationships that stultify citizenship. Adding democratic elements to established models that have anti-democratic elements does not create a democratic culture. It simply camouflages anti-democratic actions. Changes must be more integrated, encompassing, and thorough. A better path encourages civic activity as a means to change fundamentally—not just mediate between—economic relations and state procedures. If democratic civic society is to exist, it must challenge and integrate its methods into these other realms.

This partitioning of realms in Barber's definition of a strong civil society emanates from his understanding of individual personality within his straight-jacket definitions of democratic models. Barber argues against the existing democratic models because they do not capture the multiplicity of interests that each citizen demonstrates. Instead, each model categorizes the citizen as either consumer or kinsman. Barber's civic society allows citizens to express what he views as their multiplicity of identities. Again, though, the question is, Do citizens have multiple identities or do they act differently given the different environments? An alternate conception is that the attributes of a strong civic culture allow the democratic personalities of a society's citizens to express themselves. Civic citizens only have one identity, that of a democratic disposition. In turn, civic elements must be applied to contractual relations and state action. Only then will all of society act democratically, and only then will people act as the authentic source of power. I would argue that citizens object to the modern idea that they must act differently in economic, state, and civic relations. Citizens do not want to display separate identities for separate realms. Instead, they would rather apply their understanding and compassion, some rational pragmatism, and an ongoing determinable balance between civic and private interest to all their activities, whether economic, political, or social. In turn, they argue for the same treatment from business and government, just as they would from their neighbors and families. Citizens act as indifferent, bottom-line consumers and passive, inept constituents because business and government cater to them and subject them in this fashion. A strong democratic civil society must not encourage different identities for different realms; it must encourage a democratic civic approach to all realms.

Claude Fischer and his co-authors provide potent examples of the interrelationship between civic life, economic activity, and public policy. In fact, their research reveals the American acceptance of a host of public choices that affect how Americans live on a daily basis. These choices determine the social and economic make-up of families and neighborhoods, and yet they are so ingrained in American ideology that they are beyond questioning. The authors, who write to counter the biological arguments advanced in *The Bell Curve*, cite the preferences afforded the middle classes and the wealthy in homeownership, and specifically, housing discrimination against African-Americans, health care protection, and tax deductions for children. For instance, since homeownership seems ingrained as part of the American dream, and since numerous ancillary businesses benefit when Americans begin to furnish and service their homes, owning a home has a privileged position in society. However, the mortgage interest deduction granted by law favors those who have more money. As Fischer and his co-authors note:

A person too poor to buy a house receives no housing subsidy . . . while a wealthy homeowner with a mansion and a vacation house may receive a subsidy worth tens of thousands of dollars. . . . If United States tax policy treated mortgage expenses the same way it treats other living expenses, like food, rent, cars, or clothes . . . , the government would have far greater revenues. Policy experts thus refer to deductions like mortgage interest as "tax expenditures," an awkward term, but one that accurately indicates that tax deductions cost the government money—which is to say that *they cost other taxpayers money*. . . . By the early 1990s, the cost of the mortgage interest and property tax deductions amounted to more than $60 billion annually, over four times as much as was spent on direct housing assistance for low-income families.[3]

To this point, the simple message is that economic policy and state action encourage specific social lifestyles. Civil society does not function in a vacuum, and thus to develop civic activity the government must either legislate or induce business to accept these preferred choices.

By preferred choices I do not mean collective choices. This is the crux of Fischer's and his co-authors' research. For while my emphasis is to recognize that civic society cannot flourish without government support and business beneficence, Fischer's principal argument is that a host of invisible public policies grant privileged positions to certain classes, thereby increasing inequality by denying equal benefits to all classes. By invisible they mean social policies that are taken for granted and do not come under significant public or governmental scrutiny. The authors extend their analysis beyond the individual and the family to corporate subsidies and government indirect aid to many private firms. Again, Fischer and his co-authors report:

Perhaps the best-known subsidies are those to farmers. . . . While the programs were designed originally to help low- and moderate-income family farmers, large-scale farmers and agribusiness are the big winners. The Progressive Policy Institute, in a report [with] the libertarian Cato Institute and the conservative Heritage Foundation, estimated that cutting, not eliminating, such agricultural subsidies would save $31 billion over five years. . . . Overall, the Cato Institute estimates that "at least 125 separate programs providing subsidies to particular industries and firms" cost the taxpayers some $85 billion per year. Analysts recognize the need for

vital national investments—building highways and bridges, constructing irriga-
tion systems that aid agribusiness, supporting research and development in start-
up industries, funding mass transit. But they argue that most existing subsidies
soak up resources that would otherwise go to productive investment, public or
private. Current federal subsidies to industry are mostly historical legacies of no-
longer-pressing problems . . . or are responses to lobbying by powerful interest
groups.[4]

If favoring corporate America were not enough, Fischer points to the
conservative Kevin Phillips's research on Reagan era federal tax policy to
show the advantages given to the wealthy. They note that while the federal tax rate for the median American family increased less than one percent from 1980 to 1990, from 23.7 to 24.6 percent, the federal rate for the
wealthiest wage-earner fell nearly nine percent, from 35.5 percent in 1980
to 26.7 percent in 1990.[5] By the end of the 1980s, then, Reagan tax policy
created a relatively flat tax rate between the average American family
income and all those Americans who earned more than the median amount.
The idea of a progressive tax on income had been reduced dramatically,
and nearly eliminated.

By the very title of their book, *Inequality By Design*, Fischer and his co-
authors contend that America privileges certain lifestyles and specific
classes and businesses through public policy and taxpayer money. Given
the cautious nature of the American electorate, especially in regard to tax-
ing and spending its money, many of these "by design" policies are not
open to public examination. Thus, a gulf exists between federal action and
public consent, which tends to make most citizens even more suspicious
and hostile toward national politics and politicians. Within the last decade,
too, this distrust and open questioning has been felt by multinational corporations as citizens begin to react in anger to these publicly financed but
socially and civilly denuding policies.

In regard to civic life, my concern is how to establish or sustain America's
civic health if significant amounts of taxpayer money are privileged to firms
and individuals with no civic connection. Moreover, it is readily apparent
why civic life has diminished if we consider the growing biases that emas-
culate society. Corporate subsidies and the concentration in wealth encourage displacement from local, community activities. Crime, welfare, and
drugs become someone else's problems as the wealthy cordon themselves
off from these concerns. Civic differentiation is also the apparent result of
this increasing inequality. As the rich get richer, as corporate subsidies grow,
as the middle classes feel a financial squeeze and are forced to have both
parents work, and as the poor simply do without, it is obvious that the

policies now in place do not encourage a healthy civic interaction with an abiding interest in political activity. Finances become the source of family discussion and marriage trouble, and civic life becomes a privileged activity as meeting payments and satisfying bills are the nerve-wracking focus. Again, the civic life that Tocqueville witnessed years ago still exists in America, but it exists in the upper-class communities. In those depressed areas, or in many suburban neighborhoods, satisfying life's necessities displaces civic interaction and community networking. As I have hinted, it seems only when communities face extreme impoverishment or extinction do some of them find their civic ability, and those areas are the ones that find their way into print. The extinct communities do not make the news.

My message, then, is that presently civic life is more an interesting national discussion promoted by those who benefit from the policy choices in place than it is a viable and likely agenda for change as it would immediately affect those who emphasize its paucity. Also, its existence today is often reflected in the social extreme: the affluent still network and interact as societal leaders while the less wealthy scramble to maintain the basic securities of life. When it does exist among those least well-off, civic life seeks simply for the community to survive, with little hope for it to thrive. Finally, if civic life is an essential component for a more vigorous democratic experiment, then its nurturance must come from the business community and from government resources that act to support the citizen initiative. Support, of course, does not mean to subject or to determine. Civic life demands citizen action first.

THE FIRST CHANGE

Despite the privileges public policy affords some groups and despite the obstacles that civic differentiation describes, civic life persists in voluntaristic and inclusive detail. However, given the aforementioned policies and in the American tradition of pursuing our lofty ideals, we can be even more civic-minded than we are. Considering this, the first change comes from meeting the challenges of everyday life and attacking the inequalities that public policy fosters. These challenges cause many to pause and refrain, as they seem too insurmountable and the differences in money, power, and prestige too large to confront. With an ever-dwindling piece of the pie, many simply decide that their piece, however less than it once was, is still relatively more than what they have had or what others now have. The first necessary change, then, that encourages a more civic culture is a change in attitude. For as David Mathews noted earlier, when people begin to see an opportunity for influence, not necessarily the likelihood of change, then they start to act.

This inertia is perhaps more powerful than any of the other obstacles people face. Some argue that the modern economy and the inventions of bureaucracy and administration are powerful conforming tools. They encourage people not only to think of their personal interests first but also to become passive subjects to the abstract and arcane issues of tax policy, welfare tests, and corporate subsidies. By entrusting others to solve these complex issues, citizens today check their results by monitoring their wallets and checkbooks. A small increase, no matter the increase for others, usually fosters a passive and accepting response. In short, to call for a healthy civic life demands a collective de-programming initiative. Citizen action first needs to acquaint people with its tacitly accepted public choices, and these choices, when under the bright light of public scrutiny, would change. The population's passivity benefits those who reap the privileges of today's policy design. Thus, greater public participation necessitates a new socialization process—and therefore a new educational emphasis—while it would likely generate class conflict. A greater public discussion about how to address fundamental issues of justice and fairness would emerge, in the Rousseauean sense of affirming first principles and not devolving into the administering of government. Or, instead of viewing these changes as decisively altering American society, these changes in education, toward inclusive decision-making participation, and in attaining societal goals are best viewed as finally meeting American ideals.

These are high demands, but a democratic civic society establishes higher standards than those we have assumed today. However, if a strong civic life demands a collective attitudinal change, the question is, How does this change occur? Citizens cannot simply alter ingrained behavior and beliefs toward their role in politics, their apparent hostility toward the federal government, and a general acquiescence to business ethics and corporate policies. The answer is that change need not be revolutionary, but it needs to emphasize the importance of public involvement and public decision-making. Thus, the fundamental concern is one of education—one of an active education toward citizenship—as well as the demonstrated linking between all societal realms. Government needs to initiate and implement educational changes—in a sense to prod individuals toward citizenship—to help begin the task. In return, the benefits that accrue from a public education and the ability to become citizens demand a degree of service.

Barber emphasizes the importance of service today, not only for its citizenship-building capacities but for its ability to foster what many critics claim America now lacks: a sense of national unity and commitment to some public goals or ideals. He gives examples of programs initiated by both government agencies and non-profit organizations that seek to upgrade the value of civic education in basic school curriculum. With a greater importance placed on the requirements and responsibilities of citizenship through the high school years, a change in attitude might be possible. Given today's climate for government constraint, he cautions against any government-led initiative. Rather, a partnership between various local, state, and national organizations, with control at the immediate level, seems politically feasible. Maryland, for instance, has instituted mandatory community service programs at the high school level. To advocates like Barber, programs that combine education and civic life are essential steps toward building a more robust civil society.[6]

The agreement is that citizens receive a public education in return for service and commitment to their society. This seems an honest compact between the citizen and the public as it makes note of the relationship between the individual and the collectivity. In this non-draft era, it establishes the oft-heard call—from both the Left and the Right—that rights must come with duties. One earns one's right to participate by giving. It also recognizes the benefits of developmental democracy in that only through practice do people learn to become citizens. As Rousseau states that wills cannot be represented and as Tocqueville argues that participation enlarges the heart and the mind, engagement allows citizens to understand the value of their participation, of others' ideas, and, in the end, of the necessity of compromise. Finally, what this change shows is the necessary interaction between all social realms, as citizens cannot undergo a collective change without government initiative and economic rethinking. A winner-take-all, zero-sum politics and a bottom-line economics has little concern for all of society's members. In an inclusive, democratic society, however, all of society's members determine the value of such political and economic thinking.

Ultimately, the vision is to give people a political voice. This entails the processes of providing greater access to the political system for American citizens. It means reducing the power of privilege and money, status and incumbency. But before I note specific national political changes, people find their political voice through the Jeffersonian legacy of practice, the kinds of political practice that occurs in communities nationwide today but goes unrecognized or under-appreciated by national policy makers and national media. Yet while people practice their democratic skills, a significant number of obstacles hinder their voice. These obstacles are more important than any governmental or business changes that can be imagined, for these changes foster greater democratic control. When the people have the ability to decide for themselves how they want their communities, then government and business must follow suit. So, in the end, the essential changes emanate from the individual and how individuals assume their democratic roles.

The present obstacles to developing a truly democratic society always come back to matters of justice and equality. Liberty seems well-protected these days, as conservatives bemoan the rights granted criminals, "marginal" groups, and the needy; liberals decry the corporate welfare granted business; business laments the privileges granted environmental groups or governmental regulation in general; and so on. However, it is when the exercise of one's liberty constrains the exercise of another's that equality becomes an issue, and in a democratic society, how we define equality is open for input from all the members of the society. Thus, rough equality need not be the result, as long as all members have the opportunity and the ability to contribute to the collective decision. With this in mind, Robin Garr discusses many of the individual needs necessary to satisfy a rough equality to meet the social contract obligation of allowing each to give input into the democratic decision-making process. With several examples of local organizing, he explains in detail how communities are addressing the most basic needs for their members. Before becoming active citizens, people need meaningful, productive employment. Before finding these jobs, people need to learn valuable, marketable skills. Before they can learn these skills, people require food, housing, and a relatively safe environment where they can focus their energies on more than just meeting life's bare necessities. Garr concludes:

> The most effective grassroots initiatives . . . return to several basic premises: Changing people's lives is labor-intensive work. . . . It's necessary to work one-on-one with people. . . . It takes competent, creative, and honest people to run successful programs . . . and they have to be left pretty much alone in order to do it. . . . But the most important lesson we learn at America's grassroots is this: Even the most apparently intractable groups of people in poverty are composed mostly of decent folks who just want a chance to make a living and support themselves and their families. If you give them a reasonable chance to work their way out of poverty . . . just about everyone will grab for it. . . . These grassroots innovations are not based on the inventions of office-bound bureaucrats or policy gurus but on the commonsense ideas of everyday Americans who've seen a problem and pitched in to help fix it.[7]

Garr's message reaffirms the worn political cliché that the entire civic virtue debate misses: all politics is local. In turn, all efforts at civic building must be local, and to involve state and national governments in these endeavors is to develop support systems only, and not to invoke some pre-established, uniform tenets that merely provide an easy flow of paperwork. Garr points to several guiding principles from the hundreds of successful programs he researched, and his principles in general call for flexibility in operation, a holistic approach that integrates as much of the community as possible, and a widespread partnership between several supportive agencies, including local, state, and federal groups. It is obvious these successful principles of grassroots organizing conflict with today's processes of bureaucracy and agency control. The idea is to entrust democracy in the local people and their methods, not in a distant professionalized class. This approach does not suggest that the ends justifies the means, but merely that the means must be flexible enough to adjust to meet both changing means and changing ends. A homeless veteran has a different set of problems to address than a homeless, illiterate mother of two. While both are homeless, providing them with the resources to develop productive lives demands different strategies and involves different constituencies.

If these changes appear too improbable, if these new attitudes and practices cannot overcome established practices, if they require too much change in American ideology and in America's well-worn customs, the numerous examples that Garr, Barber, and other authors and researchers cite could not exist. In fact, these new attitudes and practices are not new at all. They evolve from Tocqueville's insights about America generations ago. They have been replaced by more efficient and, in some ways, more equal methods of adjudicating between different interests. These more recent methods provide one system of addressing complex issues in a democratic polity. However, they constitute but one way of tackling modern problems. Even participatory nay-sayers, who invoke the issue of size when confronting democratic deliberation and decision-making, must admit that technology and communication offer an entirely new set of possibilities to disseminate information, transfer ideas, and promote inclusion. One of the lessons from Jesse "The Body" Ventura's startling 1998 gubernatorial election victory in Minnesota was his use of the Internet to compensate for his lack of funds as a third party candidate. While he employed a relatively new medium for the dissemination of his political ideas, he also catered to the long-heralded disinterested, disenfranchised set—the 18- to 24-year olds. The idea is that democracy requires ongoing interest to reflect the

ongoing changes society, government, and business all collectively produce. The process of involvement, like democracy itself, is only satisfied
when it is ongoing. Much like Garr's principle in addressing poverty and
homelessness, democracy is a labor-intensive effort. Besides labor, it also
demands a fine balancing act between people and systems, between the
human touch and the established procedure. It is this difficult balancing
that necessitates continual assessment and participation.

CORPORATE CIVICS

If Barber confuses us with his definition of civil society, his remedies
for present society recognize the interconnectedness of all social realms.
In *A Place for Us*, he outlines six broad areas that demand legislative attention to construct a stronger civic society. Two of these areas are far-reaching attempts to control how economic production and consumption operate. He seeks greater control over corporate action by demanding more
from them, not only through government regulation but through citizen
activity. He also requires greater protections for the labor market, and
greater awareness about society's consumptive habits and their consequences. Moreover, Barber understands the social implications of the free
reign granted to business. In contrast, he argues:

> Responsibility and power go hand in hand: nothing has greater power today
> than a multinational corporation; no group has been left with less responsibility.
> . . . The new moralists who applaud the containment of government like to make
> vigorous civic demands on pregnant children and unemployed immigrants; they
> might more appropriately make them on Time-Warner and Microsoft. We rightly
> ask whether schools adequately provide for the moral education of children. We
> also have the right to ask whether Disneyland and MTV and the mall do the same.
> . . . In an ideal world I would prefer to have democratic government enforce public
> standards and leave corporations to the business of productivity and profit-taking;
> in the world we actually live in, the predicate for reestablishing a robust civil soci-
> ety is a new civic compact that specifically obligates corporations.[8]

Recognizing that corporations induce demand and attempt to monopo-
lize supply, that they seek ever lower labor costs, and that they exercise
undue power over political choices and social conditions reveals the strange
position American business has in society and with government. On one
hand, the antagonism between business and government represents the
fine balance between corporate liberty and government's protection of the
public interest. Government regulation restricts the freedom to earn a living and make a profit. The free market must have few restrictions to allow

the consumer to determine supply and demand. This antagonism, today, still receives most of the airplay and news coverage.

On the other hand, what we often fail to recognize are the mutual interests that corporations, government, and society share. In many other Western economies, a project of shared cooperation in achieving production and distribution goals replaces America's hostility and conflict. To be sure, some of these countries limit economic competition, while America views competition as the best method to ensure the best product and price for the consumer. But another one of Barber's realities is that multinationals undercut their competition to drive them out of business. Also, it is common sense that those companies who offer the best price rarely offer the best quality service or product. The idea here is that the antagonistic relationship between corporate America and government regulation—in essence between liberty as license and liberty with social constraints—highlights a tension that occurs increasingly less today as government and industry often work together. It receives the most airplay because it notes an enduring historical conflict. But it is a conflict that occurs with less frequency in contemporary corporate-political relations. Microsoft's notoriety gained from Justice Department accusations of illegal business practices, are in part due to this fundamental distinction between the firm's supposed free market exercises and the public's protection through vigorous competition. But the sensationalism surrounding the case forms also from the mere fact that business and government rarely find themselves in such hostile, opposed camps.

Furthermore, theoretically the conflict between business and government misapplies the understanding of the social compact and the proper relationship—which conservatives often seek to reestablish—between rights and the public good. Business will always rail against any intervention that hinders its ability to make its product or deliver its service as it freely wishes. But the fundamental issue is that corporate behavior, given its legally enshrined status as American citizens, demands citizenship obligations. Citizenship, then, entails a social contract of responsibilities that come with the ability to exercise one's economic pursuits. Some of these responsibilities, as the last few decades reveal, entail greater environmental monitoring, a more involved role in the health of a business community, and leadership roles which represent a company's significant power and influence in local issues. In these cases, liberty exercises responsibility and not license. The freedom to conduct business recognizes that first a prior social contract allows a firm to pursue its business opportunities. Only from a prior agreement does a business have the freedom to operate. In return for this freedom, a duty exists to satisfy those ideals and practices that are also essential components of the social contract. At base, freedom only comes from the social agreement to encourage free activities. Because this agreement also demands responsibilities, just as citizens cannot yell "Fire" in a crowded theater, corporate actions require social good assessments.

Assessment typically falls to government action. However, with greater community involvement and citizen activity in public affairs, citizens are integral participants to assess corporate behavior. Also, limits exist when comparing corporate activity and citizen activity, simply because corporations exert much more influence than nearly all citizens. Given their resources and their employees' dependency, business actions need greater scrutiny than ever. Accordingly, a more radical proposal that incorporates active citizenship and business accountability to a set of specific responsibilities involves the ongoing public assessment of corporate charters. While seemingly politically impractical, citizens already monitor corporate activity and wage political battles against some notorious practices. To name just two popular examples, Nike's and Kathie Lee Gifford's clothes lines have been cited for their subcontractors' use of child labor and their long work hours and low wages. A few years ago, the Nestle corporation was denounced for its promotion of tainted baby formula in third world countries, and many firms and universities were forced to divest from South Africa because of its apartheid practices. Citizens have checked the growth of nuclear power, demanded greater concern for consumer issues, and called attention to a multitude of local concerns, from urban sprawl to community policing, that check business actions and affirm the power of the community.

What makes citizen review of corporate charters radical is that citizenship itself is not reviewed once it is granted. The change in outlook is that since businesses exert significant influence in a community—whether by receiving tax breaks or by providing a business ripple effect from job growth, public school growth, and extra necessary public services—their practices need to conform to a clearly-stated social agenda. As individuals learn to become involved and effective citizens, companies learn similar lessons. Several dramatic changes come with citizen review, such as the ability to restrict companies from leaving a community and the ability to apply putative measures on firms if they fail to meet the public agenda. The intent is to control corporate power by allowing democratic citizenship the ability to evaluate its activities. One way to view corporate action is to compare it to how we treat welfare recipients. More frequently we demand means-testing to prove one's need for social services. If we demand more from the poor and needy to benefit from public goods, we also should expect multinationals to prove how they satisfy even higher social standards from their privileged positions. This proposal evolves from the historical understanding that to grant a corporate charter meant to create a firm that would serve a public function and secure a public good. Today, we understand firms best as private operations designed to make a profit. A citizen review connects this historical view with today's operation.

While dramatic changes such as corporate citizen review seem sensible but improbable, more likely avenues of change will emerge from the ongoing attention by an active, mobilized citizenry. In a sense, if citizenship begins to change, perhaps egged on with governmental support and initiative, then a vision of once improbable changes will emerge. An informed and participatory electorate easily can check how firms function. If differences emerge between the public good and the firm's actions, and industry does not have the escape options that are common in today's global marketplace, then firms will begin to respect the public will. Yet, while this level of conflict is possible, the intention is to encourage conciliation and to establish mutual agendas. Just as differences exist in a participatory political process, the motivation for government, business, and citizens is to find common ground that can provide for some satisfaction of everyone's goals. If no commonality is possible, the citizenry needs to make an informed collective decision. Certainly, this proposal glosses over many expected and unexpected problems, but the idea is to restore a greater balance in the decision-making process to the citizenry. If society chooses a democratic form of social compact, then it must decide—with input from the relevant sources—how post-industrial, high-technology capitalism must function within this democracy. At base, since today's practice of economic freedom has produced ever greater inequalities—inequalities that hinder democratic expression—a fundamental change in economic thinking must occur. While viable alternatives exist, the main point is that citizens must exert the time and effort to choose how they want to design and live a more humane and just economic contract.

THE ESSENTIAL GOVERNMENT

It should come as little surprise that in my analysis government is both an accomplice to nefarious actions and a refuge for the public interest. Government's size and its variety of functions expose it to both praise and blame. I have described it as sometimes business's accomplice by legislating inequality. Other times it is a positive initiator and a viable resource for citizen action. This apparent duality again reveals the complexity of attaining civic virtue. A multiplicity of views exists, all with different methods and ideas concerning government's function. Yet, most seek to achieve some balance between individual freedom and community responsibilities.

For the most part, two arguments underscore my approach. The first is that economic inequality is the principal culprit for America's social problems, and a greater concern for those who receive less in and from society would immediately reduce any discussion about a dearth of civic virtue. In addition, despite these favorable practices that allow business to grow wealth and the rich to become richer, civic virtue still exists in the most oppressed communities. It is as if even in the darkest times the human spirit finds something—and usually that something is the connection of community—to sustain itself. A second argument reiterates a well-worn thread these days. Since business exerts tremendous power in both the political process and society in general, citizens must be given greater avenues to claim their political voice and assert their abdicated powers. From these arguments, it seems that business is the source of societal problems and a scourge that needs rectifying. Also, the people are the resource for addressing these problems and controlling business's effects.

This scenario, along with the aforementioned duality attributed to governmental action, provides a nebulous scope for government's role. If citizens assert their democratic role as *the* repository of power while they continue to maintain an active, engaged effort to collectively address social issues, then government's role seems uncertain. However, given the complexity of modern issues and the sheer size of business operations and social concerns, government certainly needs to maintain a sizable capacity for oversight, regulation, and, in the activist tradition, initiation. As Garr explains, though, what makes a local program successful is local control and flexibility. Government initiatives often tend toward bureaucratizing the program and stifling creativity and openness. In turn, accounting for a government program's worth needs change, as feeding the hungry and housing the homeless remains a labor-intensive and not just a capital-intensive effort. Lisbeth Schorr makes this point when she claims that most of the successful social local programs she researched a decade ago have now been co-opted and made ineffectual by the federal government's dominance. In assessing programs that address children and family issues, she repeats many of the same necessary characteristics that Garr cites. Not only must programs be flexible and deal with people in their contextual circumstances—meaning familial and neighborhood relationships—but they must be run by competent, rule-bending leadership with trained, skillful staffs, all of whom nurture a trusting environment. These characteristics are hardly the image that people have of a federal government initiative.

In fact, Schorr emphasizes that what breeds success is the contingency of the program's operation. Contingency, that is, in the sense of finding out what is successful in that particular area with those specific people and acting on that success. She states that the Council of State Policy and Planning Agencies concluded, "'Successful programs recognize and respond to the needs of the community; they reflect the character of the people, . . . they build capacity in people and in neighborhoods.' . . . The Council concluded that 'best practices' are whatever works in a given context."[9] Contingency does not mean the lack of a definitive mission. Rather, from her research, Schorr uncovers a central paradox that plagues the interaction of federal programs and local initiatives. One of the most common characteristics that separate the successful programs from others was the willingness of the participants, especially leaders like school principals, to break the established rules. She then argues that when successful plans "confront the traditional sources of financing, accountability, governance, and public perception,"—in effect, when smaller plans are scaled up—these flexible, changeable plans fail to affect the larger systems that now control their fate.[10] The paradox is that what works at the smaller level never has the opportunity to succeed at a larger scale because the processes in place mute the beneficial traits necessary for success. In a sense, size breeds uniformity, but success demands creative differences and special circumstances.

Schorr's research reiterates important lessons for governmental change in general. The import of Jefferson's legacy, which evolves also from Rousseau's disdain for representation, is that local issues must be controlled locally. If the scale extends to the federal level, then a host of problems emerge. A trade-off exists when the federal government works at the local level. The benefits are the wealth of additional resources available, funding being the most obvious one. However, with the federal government comes a plethora of rules and regulations to ensure a host of other well-meaning but perhaps inapplicable or burdensome requirements to that specific need. The government must guarantee demands for equality in assessing need and delivering a service. It must establish inclusive means of hiring and promoting greater employment opportunities for certain peoples. These additional requirements, while socially desirable, have the unlikely effect of overburdening the once successful local program. In a sense, we are inhibiting our own success by trying to ensure our established values and ideals.

If our values and ideals trip up our efforts to solve our problems, the change necessary is not the oft-repeated libertarian and conservative chant of stripping the federal government from our everyday lives. The solution is to allow the citizens to decide how they want their government to act. Sometimes the government can be an initiator of policy, and thus it must have the resources available to act in a national capacity. Other times, it must play the role of supporter, much like a foundation acts to provide money and guidance, but not direction and oversight. Finally, it must also allow communities to act for themselves. As people learn how to act and think as citizens, one result will be a changing role, one of greater variety and responsiveness, for the federal government. It cannot disappear from everyday American life, simply because it needs to protect the public interest from the possible actions of business. Although, some of its roles must be decided by each locale's engaged citizenry.

This is not to say, as Alan Ehrenhalt infers, that society suffers from the changes of the last thirty to forty years. Ehrenhalt, in both *The United States of Ambition* and *The Lost City*, bemoans the federal presence and the emergence of career politicians. He recognizes that while the Chicago neighborhoods of the 1950s are a time and a place America cannot and probably should not recapture, he writes of the interest and the feeling of community, security, and trust that has been lost. With the growth of more democracy, in his mind, comes political stalemate and policy ineffectiveness. For Ehrenhalt, the question is often reduced to whether America prefers yesterday's certainty with its inequities to today's uncertainties with its penchant for single-issue clamoring and tiring tirades for the latest oppressed group.[11] However, Ehrenhalt's either-or, black-white images do not provide the colorful complexity that this fundamental issue raises. While he argues less for a time gone by than for values lost, he fails to see that trust and community are still prevalent today, only outside his notions of the traditional family and the business leadership. Also, as I have repeated, changing economic standards as well as changing social standards compromises the values he holds dear. In Ehrenhalt's lost America, you knew whose palm you needed to grease; accountability and responsibility were obvious and effective tools for citizen action despite the dirtiness of the activity. Today, though, accountability needs to reside in the people, where they can determine how dirty or clean they prefer their government and their politics.

In a similar vein as Schorr's paradox, the most apparent question is, Why do citizens lack political clout these days? If review after report state that only through the peoples' actions can democracy succeed, why then do changes fail or produce few lasting effects? Also, if the changes that government must undergo are patently obvious and oft-repeated, then why do these changes fail to materialize? The simple answer is that citizens do not have control of the governmental process, and while they act in heroic fashion in their communities, state and federal action remains a professional enclave that caters to a multitude of interests that can cancel out citizen sympathies. A more complex answer incorporates the political structure's distancing effects from what some label as popular whim from the rabble or the masses. It understands that the political system's checking mechanisms allow for maintenance and status quo more than change. It also recognizes the unimaginable unequal influence on political leaders by the economic system and its leaders. Local democracy shows that many participants can be active in politics; national representation shows that politics often comes down to a few players with self-interested agendas. Finally, and by no means exhaustively, democracy is another labor-intensive effort, and given the American preference and need for primarily an economic focus over the last generation or two, the effort allocated to democracy's success does not satisfy many of America's assumed aspirations. Depending on where one explores, communities meet America's values and ideals or they fail miserably. The issue is whether this mix of successes and failures placates the citizenry.

If the citizenry sees a need for change, some of the more discussed proposals include reducing the influence of money in the political process. In campaigns, rid the system of soft money, legislate for equal public air time for all candidates,—if corporations are in fact public entities, then surely networks are equally accountable—and open debates to the public instead of asking the typical questions from a panel of agreed-upon experts. Reelection rates for the 1998 U.S. House of Representatives were 98.5 percent, 395 out of 401 reelected, with winning margins of over 20 percent, which is considered landslide proportions. In 74 percent of the races, 321 out of 435. Twenty-two percent of the races went uncontested. Only five minor party candidates won seats, all of them in Vermont, from over 7,000 candidates in state elections nationwide. Overall turnout was 37 percent, distinguishing America with the lowest participation rates of any established democracy.

From these results, the most immediate concern is to increase competitiveness, simplify voting, and make the process more representative. In

1998, Arizona and Massachusetts passed referenda that will provide public financing of campaigns in state elections. Oregon approved mail-in balloting, making it easier for people to vote. As redistricting of Congressional districts by state legislatures occurs after every ten-year census, and the growth of safe seats is the most obvious result of partisan redistricting, Iowa's criteria-based redistricting plan pursues a more inclusive path less prone to party self-interest. Moreover, America's plurality voting system needs to change. Most democracies use a proportional system, where a candidate's percentage of votes translates directly to a percentage of representation. For the most significant offices, instant runoff voting is a viable alternative. This election process allows voters to list their candidates in order of preference. If no candidate wins a majority of first-choice votes, the last-place candidate is eliminated. Votes for the last-place candidate are recast to each voter's next choice, and this process of elimination occurs until one candidate has a majority. Thus, wasted votes cannot exist, independent or third party candidates are more encouraged to run, and competition increases.

In the legislative process, limit the monetary access special interests have to representatives and senators. Impose penalties on the politicians themselves if they fail to meet budget or other requirements. Responsibilities come with the office, and while some note the special power to stalemate unfavorable legislation, the consequence is inaction. If change is one of life's constants—except perhaps in Congress—then inaction does greater damage than good. Protecting one's constituents by promoting gridlock misunderstands the basic representative function: to come to a decision in the name of the public interest. Because the public interest has different meanings for different representatives does not mean that the status quo is an acceptable course of (in)action. As hasty legislation reflects poorly on Congress, no legislation reveals a lack of consensus, certainly, as well as a lack of concern for the public interest. No better example exists than the failure of federal representatives to marshal health care reform through their deliberative processes.

Just as citizens need an education process that inculcates and breeds citizenship, politicians need an attitudinal change in their roles. Perhaps if jobs in Congress paid less or provided fewer opportunities for former-Congresspeople to make enormous sums of money as post-office lobbyists and lawyers, then self-interest may play less of role in policy-making and campaigning. Since self-interest is the hallmark of Madison's seminal statement on representation in *Federalist #10*, American representation needs an overhaul. Since change most aptly characterizes society, change needs to inform government. As Jefferson noted, "On similar ground it may be proved that no society can make a perpetual constitution, or even a perpetual law. . . . The constitution and the laws of [a generation's] predecessors [are] extinguished then in their natural course with those who gave them being. This could preserve that being till it ceased to be itself, and no longer."[12] The intent is to encourage engaged citizens to fashion a government and a politics that suits them and their times. Relying on some historical document provides a valuable resource, but it also cannot address the problems associated with modern life. Only when the people are informed and active can government operate to meet society's needs. The first step, then, to engage the people, provides the means for all subsequent changes.

BALANCING AN IDEAL

My father's community service establishes a high civic standard. For some it invokes a time of stronger commitments between neighbors and trustworthiness and confidence throughout the country. Equally compelling examples appear to us in these more dangerous and defeating times. The inner-city pastor who ministers to the poor and hopeless; the indefatigable activist who never concedes defeat against land developers or absentee landlords; the bereaved parents who fight for victim's rights on behalf of lost children; the enterprising samaritan who best understands how to motivate others and rectify local inequities. The examples need not be dramatic or popular, just an endless body of citizens, interested and involved, who act daily on local concerns for the good of their communities.

But given these uncertain times filled with complex issues with unforeseen ripple effects or incalculable, distant consequences, a nostalgia clouds American thinking. At times, our thinking reminisces about a time past when towns were safe as kids played at the nearby sandlot, when people were friendlier as neighborhoods were well-defined and traditions guided behavior, and when communities were engines of democracy as citizens acted to provide a better, more productive future. However much these reveries pull at our heartstrings for simplicity and human decency, they delude more than inform our present realities. My father's actions, then, are not of value for their unique historicity. They are of value as an example of democratic practice and action: to find one or more issues to help others and help a community. For my father, and for many Americans across this country, the first words from their mouths after recognizing a social need are, "How can I help?"

From complex issues that inhibit actions and stunt concern to motivated citizens involved in each community, is there a split personality in American behavior? While at times I paint a picture of insurmountable modern-day obstacles, I also herald the innumerable examples of informed action throughout the country's communities. No permanent distinction persists, though, as many of us experience both the rewards of contributing and the purposelessness of modern life. People can feel overwhelmed by their lack of power and proud of their impact in the same day. The only way to attack the relentless forces that undermine our initiative and cause us to lose faith is to contribute and involve ourselves in activities beyond our private spaces. Interestingly, this political conclusion seems as much a religious lesson and moral adage as it does a solution to both private and public concerns. The sense of community that religious affiliation generates is one of the primary goals of civic life. However, civic life seeks this end not through a divine mediary. Rather, citizens who engage each other and recognize their power replace any mediary mechanism. Faith lies in the responsible actions of people working toward collective goals.

Concerned citizens accomplish meaningful work day-in and day-out in communities across this country. This gives us great hope for America's future and encourages more effort to tackle our pressing issues. But, as a reminder of the effort ahead, and despite my message that civic life is alive and well, change seems as much improbable as possible. For it is obvious too that power is misplaced today and the changes necessary to inculcate a more democratic system confront entrenched interests and misguided attitudes. Given the human disposition, or perhaps just the American character, that invokes caution and suspicion toward any significant change, establishing a stronger civic culture with power vested in all the people is a demanding ideal.

In addition, over the course of this century, a national unity developed domestically in response to the Great Depression and for the creation of the welfare state. Internationally, world wars followed by a policy of communist containment also contributed to a national identity. In turn, Americans ceded their power to a growing, protective government. Power was ceded because the marketplace held no social security for citizens. Business was not interested in human welfare. Consequently, with the failures of the welfare state and with the lasting effects of the Vietnam War, America is less trusting of its government and more uncertain about its grant of power. Government is too large and ineffectual, business too single-minded and harsh. While some of us long for a time of greater national unity and cohesion, the last thirty years of American politics and social change make this vision less likely.

Not all Americans, though, have retreated from the polls and from their communities. Many more than what today's national civic debate assumes epitomize the American values and ideals of democratic interaction. Many participate in Tocqueville's vital associational life, where democracy succeeds through active citizenship. At best, as political theory and democratic practice reveal, a delicate balancing act exists. Liberty must be assessed with equality, private interests monitored by public goods, and business innovation checked by citizen action and government regulation. We achieve these tenuous, evolving balances when we are citizens of our communities. Today's civic examples exude great promise for American democracy, and as with any tenuous balance, a number of changing obstacles challenge this promise. To address these obstacles, it is clear that no final end exists for citizenship, no state of perfection or attainment, only an ongoing series of interesting and fulfilling tasks, shared with others, with the lasting benefit of shared purposes.

NOTES

1. Benjamin R. Barber, *A Place for Us: How to Make Society Civil and Democracy Strong* (New York: Hill and Wang, 1998), 34–35.

2. Ibid., 48–49.

3. Claude S. Fischer, Michael Hout, Martin Sanchez Jankowski, Samuel R. Lucas, Ann Swidler, and Kim Voss, *Inequality by Design: Cracking the Bell Curve Myth* (Princeton, N.J.: Princeton University Press, 1996), 136–137.

4. Ibid., 144–145.

5. Ibid., 147–148.

6. Barber, *A Place for Us*, 106–107.

7. Robin Garr, *Reinvesting in America: The Grassroots Movements that Are Feeding the Hungry, Housing the Homeless, and Putting Americans Back to Work* (New York: Addison-Wesley Publishing, 1995), 230.

8. Barber, *A Place for Us*, 91, 94, 96.

9. Lisbeth B. Schorr, *Common Purpose: Strengthening Families and Neighborhoods to Rebuild America* (New York: Anchor Books, 1997), 7–8.

10. Ibid., 18–19.

11. For instance, see Alan Ehrenhalt, *The United States of Ambition: Politicians, Power, and the Pursuit of Office* (New York: Times Books, 1991), 270–276.

12. Thomas Jefferson to James Madison, 6 September 1789, *The Portable Thomas Jefferson*, ed. Merrill D. Peterson (New York: Viking Penguin, 1975), 449.

Selected Bibliography

Aristotle. *The Politics.* Translated by T. A. Sinclair. Baltimore, Md.: Penguin Books, 1962.

Barber, Benjamin. *A Passion for Democracy: American Essays.* Princeton, N.J.: Princeton University Press, 1998.

Barber, Benjamin. *A Place for Us: How to Make Society Civil and Democracy Strong.* New York: Hill and Wang, 1998.

Barry, Brian. *Justice as Impartiality.* Oxford: Clarendon Press, 1995.

Becker, Theodore L., ed. *Quantum Politics: Applying Quantum Theory to Political Phenomena.* New York: Praeger Publishers, 1991.

Bellah, Robert N., Richard Madsen, William M. Sullivan, Ann Swidler, and Steven M. Tipton. *Habits of the Heart: Individualism and Commitment in American Life.* New York: Harper and Row Publishers, 1985.

Bennett, William J. *The De-Valuing of America: The Fight for Our Culture and Our Children.* New York: Summit Books, 1992.

Bork, Robert. *Slouching Toward Gomorrah: Modern Liberalism and American Decline.* New York: Regan Books, 1996.

Boxx, T. William, and Gary M. Quinlivan, eds. *Culture in Crisis and the Renewal of Civil Life.* Lanham, Md.: Rowman and Littlefield Publishers, 1996.

Boyte, Harry C. *The Backyard Revolution: Understanding the New Citizen Movement.* Philadelphia: Temple University Press, 1980.

Bronfenbrenner, Urie, Peter McClelland, Elaine Wethington, Phyllis Moen, and Stephen J. Ceci. *The State of Americans: This Generation and the Next.* New York: The Free Press, 1996.

Bruton, Henry J. *On the Search for Well-Being.* Ann Arbor: The University of Michigan Press, 1997.

Caplan, Arthur L., and Daniel Callahan, eds. *Ethics in Hard Times.* New York: Plenum Press, 1981.

Cohen, Jean L., and Andrew Arato. *Civil Society and Political Theory.* Cambridge, Mass: MIT Press, 1992.

Coontz, Stephanie. *The Way We Really Are: Coming to Terms with America's Changing Families.* New York: Basic Books, 1997.

Dahl, Robert A., and Edward R. Tufte. *Size and Democracy.* Stanford, Calif.: Stanford University Press, 1973.

DeLue, Steven M. *Political Thinking, Political Theory, and Civil Society.* Boston: Allyn and Bacon, 1997.

Derber, Charles. *The Wilding of America: How Greed and Violence Are Eroding Our Nation's Character.* New York: St. Martin's Press, 1996.

Dionne, E. J., Jr. *Community Works: The Revival of Civil Society in America.* Washington, D.C.: Brookings Institution Press, 1998.

Dionne, E. J., Jr. *They Only Look Dead: Why Progressives Will Dominate the Next Political Era.* New York: Simon and Schuster, 1996.

Dionne, E. J., Jr. *Why Americans Hate Politics.* New York: Simon and Schuster, 1991.

Eberly, Don E., ed. *The Content of America's Character: Recovering Civic Virtue.* Lanham, Md.: Madison Books, 1995.

Ehrenhalt, Alan. *The Lost City: Discovering the Forgotten Virtues of Community in the Chicago of the 1950s.* New York: Basic Books, 1995.

Elshtain, Jean Bethke. *Democracy on Trial.* New York: Basic Books, 1995.

Erikson, Kai, and Steven Peter Vallas. *The Nature of Work: Sociological Perspectives.* New Haven, Conn.: Yale University Press, 1990.

Fairlie, Henry. *The Spoiled Child of the Western World: The Miscarriage of the American Idea in Our Time.* Garden City, N.Y.: Doubleday and Company, Inc., 1976.

Fischer, Claude S., Michael Hout, Martin Sanchez Jankowski, Samuel R. Lucas, Ann Swidler, and Kim Voss. *Inequality by Design: Cracking the Bell Curve Myth.* Princeton: Princeton University Press, 1996.

Garr, Robin. *Reinvesting in America: The Grassroots Movements that Are Feeding the Hungry, Housing the Homeless, and Putting Americans Back to Work.* New York: Addison-Wesley Publishing, 1995.

Gerth, H. H., and C. Wright Mills, eds. *From Max Weber: Essays in Sociology.* New York: Oxford University Press, 1946.

Giddens, Anthony. *Beyond Left and Right: The Future of Radical Politics.* Stanford, Calif.: Stanford University Press, 1994.

Giddens, Anthony. *The Consequences of Modernity.* Stanford, Calif.: Stanford University Press, 1990.

Gleick, James. *Chaos: Making a New Science.* New York: Viking Press, 1987.

Goldfarb, Jeffrey C. *The Cynical Society: The Culture of Politics and the Politics of Culture in American Life.* Chicago, Ill.: The University of Chicago Press, 1991.

Gordon, David M. *Fat and Mean: The Corporate Squeeze of Working Americans and the Myth of Managerial "Downsizing."* New York: The Free Press, 1996.

Greider, William. *Who Will Tell The People: The Betrayal of American Democracy.* New York: Simon and Schuster, 1992.

Gross, Michael L. *Ethics and Activism: The Theory and Practice of Political Morality.* New York: Cambridge University Press, 1997.

Harrigan, John J. *Empty Dreams, Empty Pockets: Class and Bias in American Politics.* New York: Macmillan Publishing Company, 1993.

Himmelfarb, Gertrude. *The De-Moralization of Society: From Victorian Virtues to Modern Values.* New York: Alfred A. Knopf, 1995.

Howard, Robert. *Brave New Workplace: America's Corporate Utopias—How They Create New Inequalities and Social Conflicts in Our Working Lives.* New York: Elisabeth Sifton Books, Viking, 1985.

Hugins, Walter, ed. *The Reform Impulse, 1825–1850*. Columbia, S.C.: University of South Carolina Press, 1972.

Janoski, Thomas. *Citizenship and Civil Society: A Framework of Rights and Obligations in Liberal, Traditional, and Social Democratic Regimes*. New York: Cambridge University Press, 1998.

Kalra, Paul. *The American Class System: Divide and Rule*. Pleasant Hill, Calif.: Antenna Publishing Co., 1995.

Kaus, Mickey. *The End of Equality*. New York: Basic Books, 1992.

Kemmis, Daniel. *Community and the Politics of Place*. Norman, Okla.: University of Oklahoma Press, 1990.

Kiel, L. Douglas, and Euel Elliott, eds. *Chaos Theory in the Social Sciences: Foundations and Applications*. Ann Arbor: University of Michigan Press, 1997.

Korten, David C. *When Corporations Rule the World*. Co-published by Kumarian Press, Inc., West Hartford, Conn., and Berrett-Koehler Publishers, Inc., San Francisco, Calif., 1995.

Kosmin, Barry A., and Seymour P. Lachman. *One Nation Under God: Religion in Contemporary American Society*. New York: Harmony Books, 1993.

Lapham, Lewis H. *Money and Class in America: Notes and Observations on Our Civil Religion*. New York: Weidenfeld and Nicolson, 1988.

Lasch, Christopher. *The Revolt of the Elites and the Betrayal of Democracy*. New York: W. W. Norton and Company, 1995.

Laski, Harold J. *The Dangers of Obedience*. New York: Harper and Brothers, 1930.

Leinberger, Paul, and Bruce Tucker. *The New Individualists: The Generation After 'The Organization Man.'* New York: HarperCollins Publishers, 1991.

Lifton, Robert Jay. *The Protean Self: Human Resilience in an Age of Fragmentation*. New York: Basic Books, 1993.

Lindblom, Charles. *Politics and Markets: The World's Political-Economic Systems*. New York: Basic Books, 1977.

Lupia, Arthur, and Mathew D. McCubbins. *The Democratic Dilemma: Can Citizens Learn What They Need to Know?* New York: Cambridge University Press, 1998.

MacIntyre, Alisdair. *After Virtue*. Notre Dame, Ind.: University of Notre Dame Press, 1984.

Masters, Roger D. *The Nature of Politics*. New Haven: Yale University Press, 1989.

Mathews, David. *Politics for the People: Finding a Responsible Public Voice*. Urbana, Ill.: University of Illinois Press, 1994.

Matthews, Richard K. *The Radical Politics of Thomas Jefferson: A Revisionist View*. Lawrence, Kans.: University Press of Kansas, 1984.

Mills, C. Wright. *The Power Elite*. New York: Oxford University Press, 1956.

Moffitt, Leonard Caum. *Connected Community: Subtle Force in a Systemic Web*. New York: Nova Science Publishers, 1996.

Montgomery, David. *Citizen Worker: The Experience of Workers in the United States with Democracy and the Free Market During the Nineteenth Century*. New York: Cambridge University Press, 1993.

Mulhall, Stephen, and Adam Swift. *Liberals and Communitarians*. Cambridge, Mass.: Blackwell Publishers, 1992.

Nagel, Thomas. *Equality and Partiality*. New York: Oxford University Press, 1991.

Peterson, Merrill D., ed. *The Portable Thomas Jefferson*. New York: Penguin Books, 1975.

Phillips, Kevin. *Arrogant Capital: Washington, Wall Street, and the Frustration of American Politics*. New York: Little, Brown and Company, 1994.

Phillips, Kevin. *Boiling Point: Republicans, Democrats and the Decline of Middle-Class Prosperity*. New York: HarperPerennial, 1994.

Phillips, Kevin. *The Politics of Rich and Poor: Wealth and the American Electorate in the Reagan Aftermath*. New York: Random House, 1990.

Putnam, Robert D. *Making Democracy Work: Civic Traditions in Modern Italy*. Princeton, N.J.: Princeton University Press, 1993.

Rauch, Jonathan. *Demosclerosis: The Silent Killer of American Government*. New York: Times Books, 1994.

Rawls, John. *A Theory of Justice*. Cambridge: Harvard University Press, 1971.

Rousseau, Jean-Jacques. *The Social Contract*. Trans. Maurice Cranston. New York: Penguin Books, 1968.

Ruthven, Malise. *The Diving Supermarket: Shopping for God in America*. New York: William Morrow and Company, Inc., 1989.

Rutman, Darrett B., and Anita H. Rutman. *Small Worlds, Large Questions: Explorations in Early American Social History, 1600–1850*. Charlottesville, Va.: University of Virginia Press, 1994.

Sandel, Michael J. *Democracy's Discontent: America in Search of a Public Philosophy*. Cambridge, Mass.: The Belknap Press of Harvard University Press, 1996.

———. *Liberalism and the Limits of Justice*, 2nd ed. New York: Cambridge University Press, 1998.

Schwarz, John E. *Illusions of Opportunity: The American Dream in Question*. New York: W. W. Norton and Company, 1997.

Seligman, Adam B. *The Idea of Civil Society*. New York: The Free Press, 1992.

Shain, Barry Alan. *The Myth of American Individualism: The Protestant Origins of American Political Thought*. Princeton, N.J.: Princeton University Press, 1994.

Sklar, Holly. *Chaos or Community?: Seeking Solutions, Not Scapegoats for Bad Economics*. Boston, Mass.: South End Press, 1995.

Skyrms, Brian. *Evolution of the Social Contract*. New York: Cambridge University Press, 1996.

Smith, Rogers M. *Civic Ideals: Conflicting Visions of Citizenship in U.S. History*. New Haven, Conn.: Yale University Press, 1997.

Soltow, Lee. *Distribution of Wealth and Income in the United States in 1798*. Pittsburgh, Pa.: University of Pittsburgh Press, 1989.

Stivers, Richard. *The Culture of Cynicism: American Morality in Decline*. Cambridge, Mass.: Blackwell Publishers, 1994.

Tester, Keith. *Civil Society*. New York: Routledge, 1992.

Tocqueville, Alexis de. *Democracy in America*. Edited by J. P. Mayer. New York: HarperPerennial, 1969.

van Parijs, Phillipe. *Real Freedom For All: What (If Anything) Can Justify Capitalism?* Oxford: Clarendon Press, 1995.

Verba, Sidney, Kay Lehman Schlozman, and Henry E. Brady. *Voice and Equality: Civic Voluntarism in American Politics*. Cambridge, Mass.: Harvard University Press, 1995.

Waldrop, M. Mitchell. *Complexity: The Emerging Science at the Edge of Order and Chaos*. New York: Touchstone Book, 1992.

Wall, Jim. *Who Speaks for God?: An Alternative to the Religious Right—A New Politics of Compassion, Community, and Civility*. New York: Delacorte Press, 1996.

Walters, Ronald G. *American Reformers 1815–1860.* New York: Hill and Wang, 1978.

Walzer, Michael. *Spheres of Justice: A Defense of Pluralism and Equality.* New York: Basic Books, 1983.

Wolman, William, and Anne Colamosca. *The Judas Economy: The Triumph of Capital and the Betrayal of Work.* New York: Addison-Wesley Publishing, 1997.

.

Index

About the Author

S. LANCE DENNING is a labor and management consultant who specializes in the complexities of business growth and workplace change. He presently is a visiting professor at Adams State College in Alamosa, CO. Among Dr. Denning's earlier publications is *The Practice of Workplace Participation* (Quorum Books, 1998).

ISBN 0-275-96459-0

EAN

HARDCOVER BAR CODE

DATE DUE
